D0319937

THE COMPLETE
LAMPSHADE KIT

THE COMPLETE LAMPSHADE KIT

100 STUNNING SHADES TO MAKE AND DECORATE

HEATHER LUKE

Little, Brown and Company
Boston • New • York • Toronto • London

PUBLISHER'S NOTE
The author and publisher have made every effort to ensure that all instructions given in this book are accurate and safe but cannot accept liability for any resulting injury, damage or loss to either person or property whether direct or consequential and howsoever arising.

A LITTLE, BROWN BOOK
First published in Great Britain in 1997
by Little, Brown and Company (UK)

Created, edited and produced by
Rosemary Wilkinson Publishing
4 Lonsdale Square, London N1 1EN

A CIP catalogue record for this book is available from the British Library.

ISBN 0-316-87928-2
(10 9 8 7 6 5 4 3 2 1)

Photography: Shona Wood
Photographic styling: Mary Stewart-Wilson
Illustrations: Stephen Dew

Printed in Hong Kong
Produced by Mandarin Offset Limited

Little, Brown & Company (UK)
Brettenham House
Lancaster Place
London WC2E 7EN

UK companies, institutions and other organisations wishing to make bulk purchases of this or any books published by Little, Brown should contact their local bookshop or the Special Sales department at the address above.
Tel: 0171 911 8000 Fax: 0171 911 8100

MEASUREMENTS
Please note that metric and imperial measurements are not exact equivalents: so for each project work in only one system. Different conversions may also be given in different projects depending on the context.

TEMPLATES
Templates throughout the book are reduced in size and printed on a grid, so that they can be enlarged to full size. The percentage of the reduction is noted on each diagram. Full-size templates for eight of the shades are also given on the loose sheet at the back of the book.

FRAMES
Standard or special frames are available by mail order from M & F Products, Wandle Mills, Bridle Path, Beddington, Croydon, Surrey CR9 4NP.

CONTENTS

6 ◆ Introduction

8 ◆ Stretched

16 ◆ Box Pleated

24 ◆ Pleated and Gathered

36 ◆ Card

48 ◆ Pinpricked and Pierced

54 ◆ Child's Play

60 ◆ Milestones

68 ◆ Tarty Party

74 ◆ Evening Dress

86 ◆ Whiter than White

96 ◆ Summer Garden

106 ◆ Pintucks and Pearls

116 ◆ Winter Warmers

122 ◆ Basic Techniques

128 ◆ Index

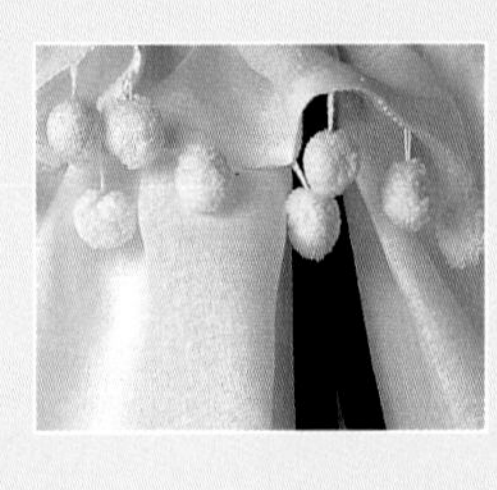

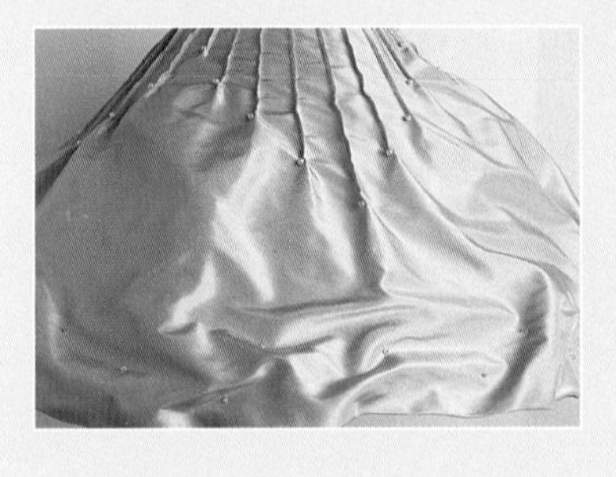

Lighting plays a vital part in setting the atmosphere of a room. Ceiling and wall lights are fixed but, fitted with dimmer switches, they can still be a flexible resource; standard lamps, table lamps and candles are portable and can be added or subtracted depending on the lighting requirements of the occasion.

The shades in this book also fall into two parts: those that are permanently fixed to the frame and those that just slip over an existing piece, providing a shade for a season or even just for one night. In the middle are card shades which feature both types: fabric-covered card shades are permanent fixtures, while the pinpricked and pierced shades and the candle shades provide instant but temporary light covers.

The fixed shades include all the traditional methods - stretched, box pleated, pleated and gathered - but with a contemporary twist through the fabrics and trimmings used. The sections on slipcovers include a wide variety of methods and materials from the simplest throwover in "Child's Play", through the stunning fabrics in "Evening Dress" to the more complex stitching methods of "Pintucks and Pearls".

Basic methods for all lampshades are given in each chapter, followed by numerous photographs of variations showing the many, many different ways these methods can be adapted and adorned to suit your room, your fabric store and the time you have available. Lampshade making can be as simple or as sophisticated as you choose and, in choosing your own shape, style and fabric, you will always have the added pleasure of producing a shade exactly suited to your own interior design sheme.

Stretched Shades

A frilled hem provides just the right amount of informality for a child's bedroom and covered seams become a decorative feature.

There's one in almost every house - a stretched, fitted lampshade often in a formal room. Such shades may look old-fashioned in their present incarnation but they can be given a new lease of life, becoming elegant in plain fabrics with contrasting trims or exuberant in florals and fringes.

Allow your sense of humour to have a subversive effect on this traditional form, interior design should never be taken too seriously! Large designs, courageously used, can be striking, especially in combination with chunky trimmings. Even a very large design will give an all-over colour impression without necessarily killing other pattern in the room, and it is better to reserve small prints for smaller shades as a tiny pattern on a big shade will just look silly.

Not only will your old shade suddenly acquire a bold contemporary look, a certain flair, but also the print and grain of the fabric that you choose will be displayed at its best when stretched over a frame. Pleating or gathering can obliterate the finely drawn motifs or characterful weave that originally caught your eye, so it is important to match the method to the materials.

There are two methods for dealing with seams on a stretched shade: I prefer the traditional one, which is to fit the fabric to the frame section by section and then to cover the joins with strips of self fabric, but it is possible to make covers which appear to be seamless. Both methods are described overleaf.

There is an enormous choice of shape for the frame, ranging from the usual square, hexagonal, round or oval to extravagant Napoleon hats or segments of pagoda.

A stretched cover can be made in two pieces or in individual sections to match the frame. Whether the cover will be made in two, four, six or eight sections, each piece of fabric will be cut on the cross. Decide how many sections you wish the cover to

have. As a general rule, the more complex the frame, the more sections you will need to be able to control the fabric. It is not really practical to make a toile (a fabric pattern) first, unless you can use exactly the same fabric, as the degree of stretch might vary between fabrics. Always work with the fabric right side outwards.

Choose fabric which has enough stretch to allow you to pull it taut, but not so much that as soon as you think it is taut, the fabric gives a little, causing bubbles. Silk dupion and linen have good grain details, fine silks might be too brittle to pull without tearing, wool and silk crêpes will need to be stretched at least twice, medium to heavyweight silks and cottons usually respond well.

YOU WILL NEED

- *prepared frame (see page 122)*
- *top fabric, see below*
- *wool or silk crêpe, for lining (see page 122)*
- *matching sewing thread*
- *curved needle (optional)*
- *PVA glue*
- *fine glue brush*
- *braid or fringing for base (optional)*

MEASURE

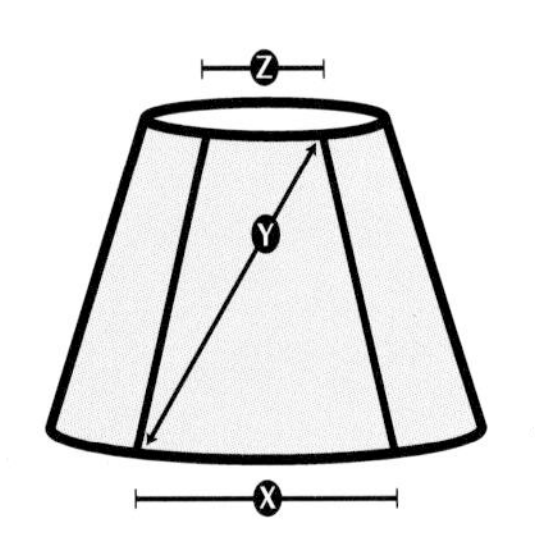

X = base of one section
Y = diagonal
Z = top of one section

Measure one section carefully, cut a rectangle of paper to this size and plan the pieces on a working surface to estimate the fabric quantity needed. Remember, the pieces are all cut on the cross. If the fabric has no napp, the pieces can be dovetailed. If self-binding the frame, allow enough fabric to make bindings with a finished width of 2.5 cm (1 in), as described on page 125.

For the seam bindings, measure one strut and add 4 cm (1½ in), then multipy this by the number of seams to be covered. The bindings are 3.5 cm (1¼ in) wide.

Traditional stretched cover

To make up

1 Measure and cut the fabric panels as described opposite. Make up and fit a tight lining (see page 122).

2 Take the first panel of the top fabric and pin to the frame, starting with one pin at each corner, then pinning at 5 - 6 cm (2 - 2½ in) intervals all round. Keep pinning in between until the fabric is pulled taut with no bubbles, creases or stretched lines. Work always from diagonal to diagonal (1).

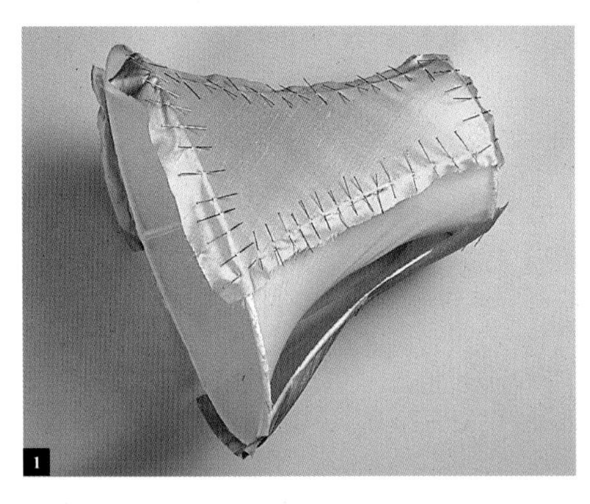
1

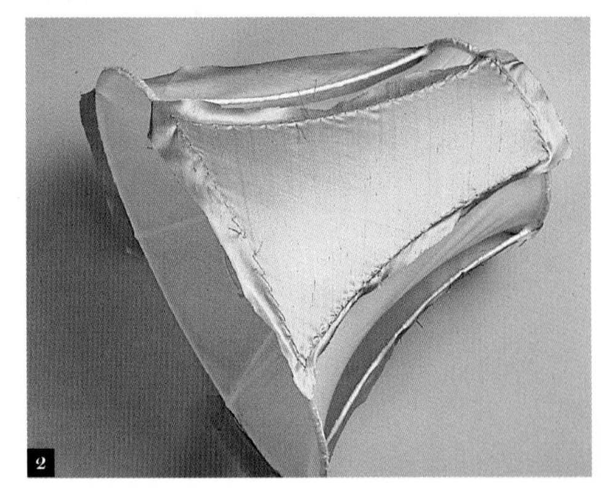
2

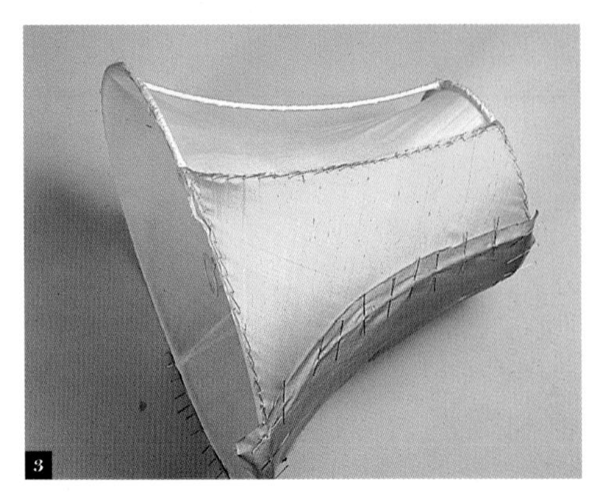
3

3 If there are only two panels, leave the shade overnight at this point to allow the fabric to rest. For four or more panels, fit the alternate panels and leave these overnight. If next day they have sagged at all, re-pin and leave to rest again.

4 Stitch the first panels securely to the bound struts with lampshade stitches 1 - 1.5 cm (⅜ - ⅝ in) in length (2). Trim the excess fabric away very close to the stitching line - the raw edges should not extend beyond the strut as any uneven edge looks very ugly when the light shines through.

5 Now continue with the remaining panels, pinning, stretching, pinning and resting as before. Stitch to the fabric beneath and through to the binding on the frame (3). Trim any excess close to the stitching line.

6 Cut strips of fabric on the cross, each 3.5 cm (1⅓ in) wide and the length of each strut plus 4 cm (1½ in). Press each lengthwise into three to make a strip 1.25 cm (½ in) wide.

7 On a small, straight shade these strips can just be secured at top and bottom but for larger and curved frames they will need to be secured against the strut. Hand stitching is possible using fine cotton and a fine curved needle but is time consuming and for the dedicated only. Keep the thread loose enough that the stitching does not make a ridge, but tight enough to hold the strip against the fabric. Glueing is the neatest alternative but you must only use an adhesive which is guaranteed not to discolour or weaken with the effects of light and time. With a very fine brush, spread a thin layer onto the centre back of one strip and along the ridge of one strut. Press the strip against the strut (4). Pin at top and bottom to hold until the glue is set. Repeat with the other strips and leave until quite dry. Trim the excess fabric.

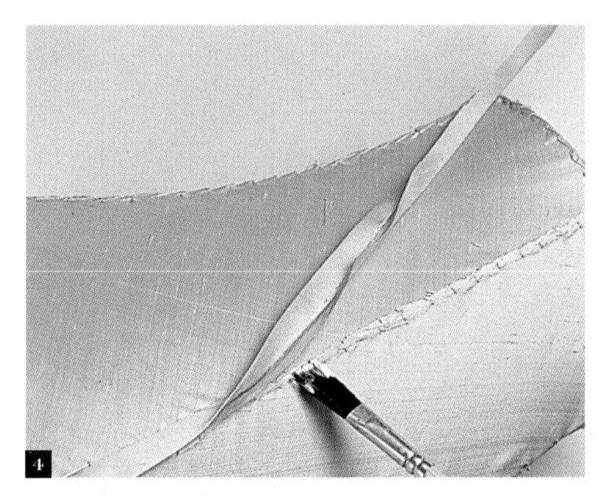

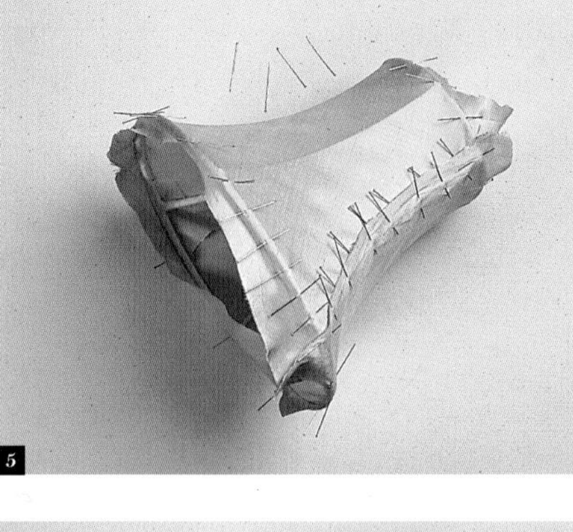

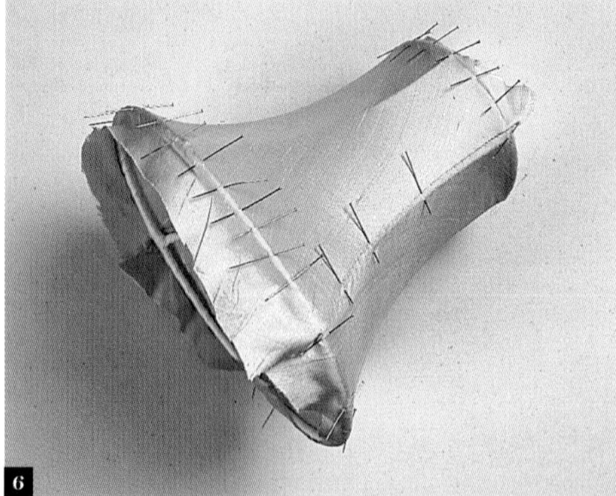

8 Finish the top and bottom with self-binding (see page 125) or with your chosen braid or fringing. These edgings should always be hand stitched in place.

Stitched seams

It is possible to make the top shade, so that the seam allowances fall on the inside. Materials and measuring instructions are the same as for the previous method.

1 Decide how many sections you wish to use for your frame, cut out and pin them to the frame following steps 1 and 3 above. Even though the cover will come off for the seams to be stitched, don't try to work inside out, since frames are rarely exactly equal on both sides (5).

2 Leave to rest and when you are happy that the sections are correctly stretched, mark the top and bottom of each seam with marking tacks, then run a light pencil mark along the seams and remove the cover from the shade. Turn inside out and pin together along the seams, lining up the marks made. Stitch together by hand with backstitch or by machine with a very shallow zig-zag stitch. This little bit of easement will prevent the fabric from tearing when it is replaced.

3 Pin the cover back onto the frame, firstly pinning each seam to the same strut, then pinning and stretching to obtain the best fit again (6). Stitch to the bottom and top of the frame with lampshade stitches 1 - 1.5 cm (3/8 - 5/8 in) long and using double thread for extra strength. Finish the frame as before.

This empire frame with scalloped edges has self-binding for the seams and top edge and is finished with a chenille fringe.

Classic linen shade in four sections

Stretching fabric onto a frame shows the grain and weave of slubbed linen at its best (*right*). Braid has been used to cover the seams and to bind the top and bottom of the frame. The braid tones with the fabric but at the same time adds a definition by introducing a strong colour, highlighting the interesting shape of the lampshade frame. The linen used here is of such quality and texture that it is as much at home in this classsic country setting, as it might be in a modern city apartment with linen sofas and neutral colours.

Adding a frilled edge to a stretched shade (above) is unusual but quite suitable in informal situations. Make up a pleated frill and pin along its raw edge to the base of the shade. Attach with lampshade stitches, then cover these with a band of self-binding.

Hexagonal frame with fringe

Deep bullion fringing is much heavier in texture and weight than the checked silk that is stretched onto this hexagonal empire frame (*above*). This juxtaposition reflects the decoration of the study in which the lamp is placed, with its rich colours and deeply textured fabrics. The shade is made in two sections with covered seams, as described on page 12.

Coolie shade

A contemporary version of the traditional stretched shade, this coolie frame (*above*) was first lined on the front with a stiff canvas to obtain a smooth round shape. Linen makes an ideal cover as its inherent strength keeps the fabric taut but its malleability enables it to be stretched round a quite steeply sloping frame.

Cut a strip of contrast fabric 10 - 15 cm (4 - 6 in) wide for the inset. Stitch it to the base and top rings, then lightly glue it to the lining underneath along each side.

Cut the cover in one piece, fit it to the top and base rings, then trim the raw edges and turn them under to reveal the inset strip.

Thread the raffia into a bodkin, then lace up the sides of the linen loosely. Pin and stitch the hems at top and bottom to the inside of the frame, then glue tape over to conceal the raw edges. Pull up the raffia tightly and tie into a bow. Finally pin strips of raffia loosely round the top and stitch in place through to the frame beneath.

Box Pleated Shades

Box pleating in silk gives a softly formal appearance to a lampshade.

As box pleats are often confused with knife pleats I have deliberately used the same shade frame covered with the same silk and the same butterfly frilled edging as at the beginning of the next chapter. The clean lines of a box pleated lampshade suit traditional and modern lighting and make this style a deservedly popular choice.

Tea caddies, spice and ginger jars in tin, ceramic and even cloisonné vases found in antique shops and markets are perfect candidates for conversion to lamp bases, as a Chinese piece will work in almost any room style. The Chinese influence on every facet of Western decorating - colours, prints, wallpapers, furniture, ceramics - is so extensive and long-established that oriental accessories seem natural in most modern day settings.

It follows that a lamp with the character and size to make it a dominant feature of a room needs a shade with a corresponding strength. And just as an oriental base will fit equally well in a white bedroom, a book-lined study or a garden room filled with overblown chintz, the shade created for it must hold its own in any situation. Just think how good both the lamp and the shade opposite would look against an ochre wall in a hallway or perhaps in a sitting room with washed denim curtains and palest aquamarine walls.

The strict geometrical nature of box pleats can fit every room style from the masculine, clubby feel to the traditionally feminine. Soften the outline of the shade with a frill, lighten its effect by using a plaid or small pattern, or allow it to make a bold statement in a richly coloured plain fabric with self-coloured binding.

Box pleats will generally not be wider than 5 cm (2 in) or narrower than 3 cm (1¼ in). They will either butt together or overlap slightly round the top of the frame. The gap between the pleats on the bottom ring is determined by the slope of the shade.

Use straight-sided frames: however, coolie style frames and those with steeply sloping sides are unsuitable, as it is almost

impossible to make enough pleats around the top so that the fabric will not run out by the time it reaches the lower ring. Just test one section of the shade with calico or muslin and experiment with pleat sizes and position, to be sure of the fullness and size of pleat which best suits your frame.

Cream silk with a slight sheen and good body is ideal for making slightly rounded box pleats. These look especially luxurious if made overlapping in a clockwise direction at the top of the shade and full enough to leave only small gaps round the lower ring. Choose patterned fabric carefully, so that motifs or geometric lines will still look good when box pleated.

YOU WILL NEED

- *prepared frame (see page 122)*
- *top fabric as chart*
- *wool or silk crêpe for lining (see page 122)*
- *matching thread*
- *self binding or braid/fringing*

MEASURE

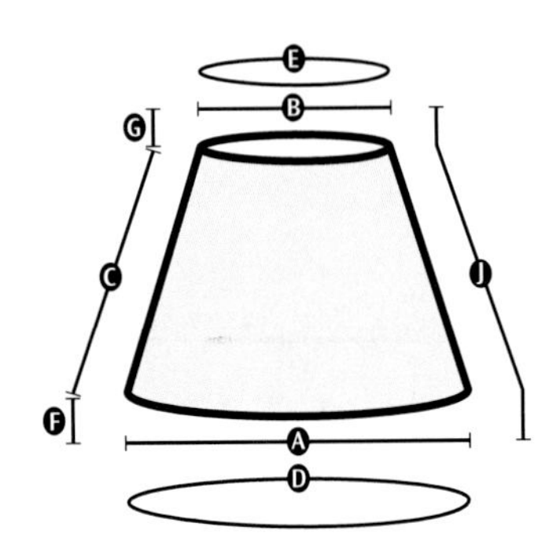

A = base diameter
B = top diameter
C = slope

Take these frame measurements, then use the chart to find fabric quantities.

STANDARD EMPIRE *(inches)*

frame size A x B x C	*fabric (3 x fullness) width x depth*	*Self binding/braid* top + base*
8 x 5 x 6	50 x 7½	42
10 x 6 x 7	60 x 8½	52
12 x 7 x 8½	68 x 10	60
14 x 9 x 10	89 x 11½	74
16 x 10 x 12	98 x 13½	84
18 x 12 x 14	116 x 15½	95
20 x 13 x 15	126 x 16½	104

PEMBROKE *(inches)*

frame size A x B x C	*fabric (3 x fullness) width x depth*	*Self binding/braid* top + base*
10 x 5 x 7	48 x 8½	50
12 x 6 x 8	60 x 9½	60
14 x 7 x 9	70 x.10½	69
16 x 8 x 10	80 x 11½	78
18 x 10 x 12	96 x 13½	90
20 x 11 x 13	110 x 14½	100

**self binding should be cut on the cross*

Box pleated shade

As a general rule, allow enough fabric to fit three times round the top. Cut the fabric in sections if necessary. There is no need to join these, as the raw edges can be invisibly incorporated into the pleats, but allow for seam allowances on each. However, if the shade has quite an exaggerated slope, then the pleats should overlap slightly along the top so that they are not too stretched round the base: up to four times the top ring can be used. Allow for self-binding the top and bottom if required.

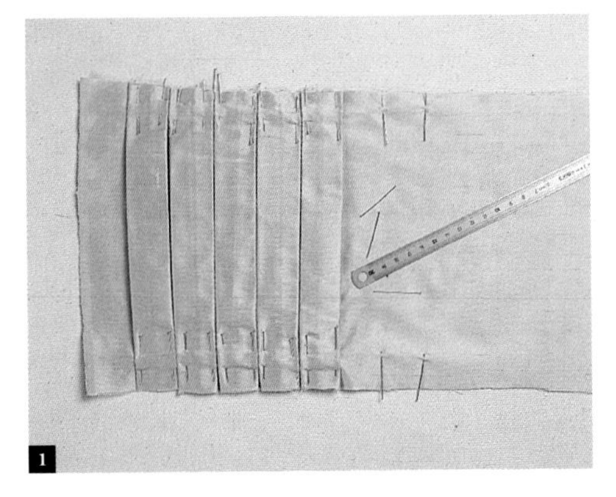
1

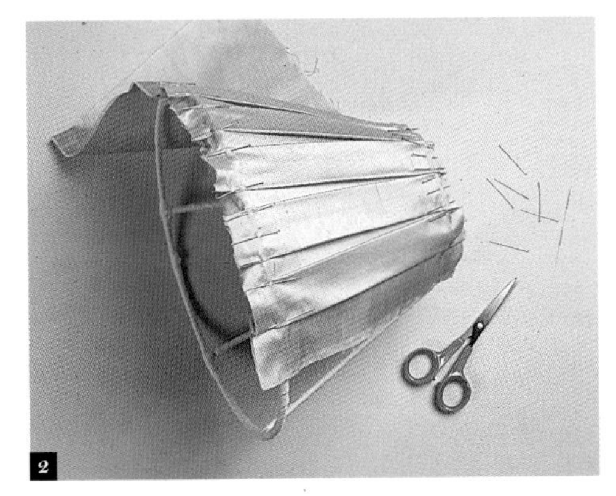
2

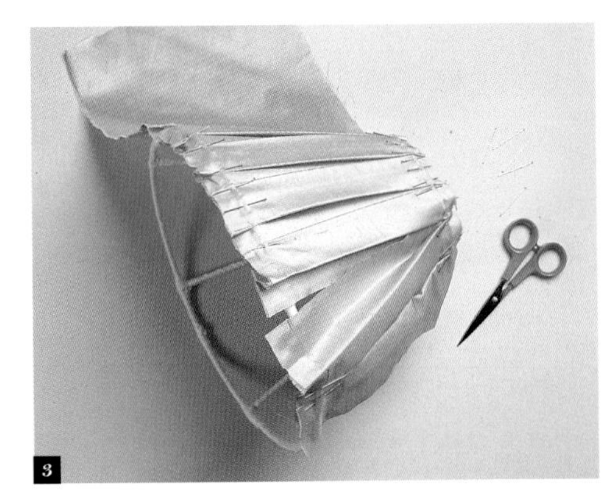
3

To make up

1 Cut the lining (see page 122) and the top fabric. Make up a pleated or tight lining (see page 122). Place one piece of the top fabric on the worktable and press to remove even the smallest crease.

2 Mark the pleat positions with pins or a light pencil (as long as you keep the marks very close to the raw edges) along both long sides. Box pleats which do not overlap need three times the finished width for each pleat, e.g. a 3 cm (1¼ in) pleat will need markings every 9 cm (3¾ in). If you find it easier, you can mark each foldline (1), i.e. every 3 cm (1¼ in), otherwise just mark the centres of each pleat.

3 Every so often check that the marks are level by running a pin along the straight of grain from top-to bottom pins. Pin the box pleats in place (1), then place this piece in position on the frame and pin securely to the top ring.

4 Keeping the pleats straight, open out each pleat at the bottom so that it fits the base ring (2). If you line up the first pleat with a strut, you will be able to use these as natural divisions. Pin in place.

5 Press, mark and pleat the next length in the same manner. Position the raw edge at the start of this section inside the last box pleat of the first as shown (3), keeping the cut edge against the fold line so that the "join" remains invisible. Continue in this way for each section, tucking the edge of the last section inside the pleat of the first.

6 Stitch each pleat to top and base rings, through all layers. Use lampshade stitches 1 - 1.5 cm (⅜ - ⅝ in) in length and double stitches on each pleat edge. Trim excess fabric close to stitching line.

7 Fit the lining, then bind the raw edges of top and bottom with self-binding as on page 125 or cover with gimp or fringe.

STANDARD EMPIRE *(centimetres)*

frame size A x B x C	*fabric (3 x fullness) width x depth*	*Self binding/braid* top + base*
20 x 12.5 x 15	127 x 19	107
25 x 15 x 18	153 x 21.5	132
30 x 18 x 21.5	173 x 25	153
35.5 x 23 x 25	226 x 29	188
40 x 25 x 30	249 x 34	213
45.5 x 30 x 35.5	295 x 39.5	241
51 x 33 x 38	320 x 42	264

PEMBROKE *(centimetres)*

25 x 12.5 x 18	122 x 21.5	127
30 x 15 x 20	153 x 24	153
35.5 x 18 x 23	178 x.26.5	175
40 x 20 x 25	203 x 29	198
45.5 x 25 x 30	244 x 34	229
51 x 28 x 33	280 x 37	254

**self binding should be cut on the cross*

All in one

A single length of fabric was used for the heading, frame and hem (*right*), allowing 18 cm (7 in) for the heading and 7 cm (2¾ in) for the hem. Machine stitch the short sides together and slip stitch the hems. Make box pleats at the top of the frame, leaving the heading allowance above the top. Splay out the pleats round the base and stitch in place. Stitch a strip of binding to the base of the frame to hide the stitches. Stitch down the heading, then scrunch it up to cover the stitches.

Beaded pleats

Pleats almost meet round the base on a frame with little slope. Pull the edges of the pleats together in the centre or at top and base, then decorate with beads, buttons or decorative embroidery stitches. Tiny pearl beads have been used on these two frames (*above*), which are self-bound at top and base.

YOU WILL NEED

- *prepared frame (see page 122): empire or straight*
- *top fabric for stretched shade and self-binding, see page 12*
- *wool or silk crêpe, for lining (see page 122)*
- *fabrics A, B and C for pleats, see below*
- *matching threads*

MEASURE

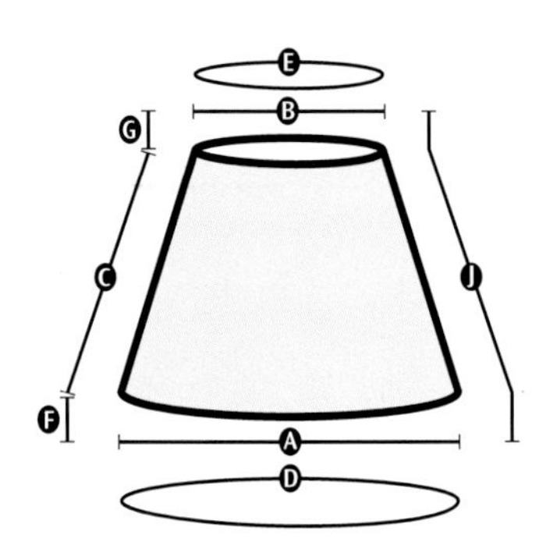

C = slope
E = top circumference

Measure the circumference of the top of the shade and divide into twelve. Each of these sections will need three pieces of fabric to make these particular mock pleats. You can use three different colours or one for A and C and a contrast for B as shown.
For an empire shade 30 x 18 x 20 cm (12 x 7 x 8 in), the following sizes can be used: back (fabric A): 8 cm (3 in) folded down to 4 cm (1½ in); centre (fabric B): 5 cm (2 in), folded to 2.5 cm (1 in); top (fabric C): 4 cm (1½ in), folded to 2 cm (¾ in).
Measure the slope, add seam allowances and cut twelve strips in each colour to this length and to the required widths.

Mock box pleats

It is possible to give the appearance of box pleats without actually pleating the fabric. This method also gives an opportunity to make the "pleats" in a different colour or a combination of colours.

To make up

1 Cover the shade following the instructions for a traditional stretched cover with stitched seams (page 13). Cut and make up a tight lining and leave aside.

2 Cut pieces of fabrics A, B and C as described left. Press each in half with the two raw edges meeting at centre back.

3 Place one each of C onto one each of B and pin, then tack together lightly all the way down and firmly along the tops and bottoms. Place this strip onto a strip of fabric A (1).

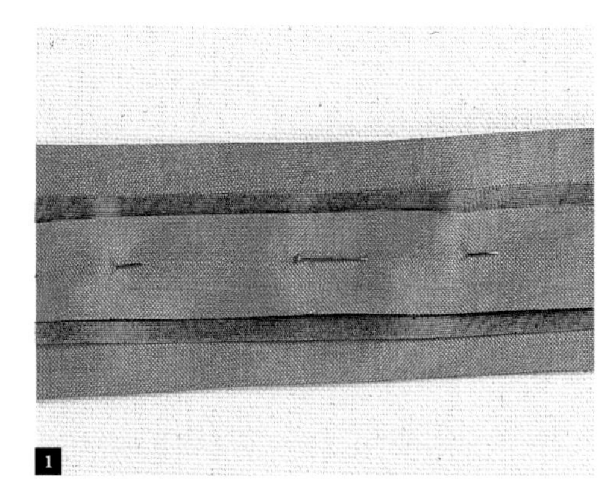
1

2

4 Pin these sections to the top and bottom of the frame and adjust so that all spacings are equal. Stitch in place securely using lampshade stitches 1 - 1.5 cm (3/8 - 5/8 in) in length. Remove the tacking threads.

5 Fit the lining, then self-bind the top and bottom to cover the raw edges (2), following the instructions on page 125.

A bandana edging of rolled silk twisted with gold and white cord (above) carries through the Italianate painted lampbase.

Single mock box pleats (left) need some kind of central definition, either simply by gathering up the pleat or by adding buttons or beads.

Pleated and Gathered Shades

Luxury and simplicity: the pleated and gathered shade is an all-time favourite.

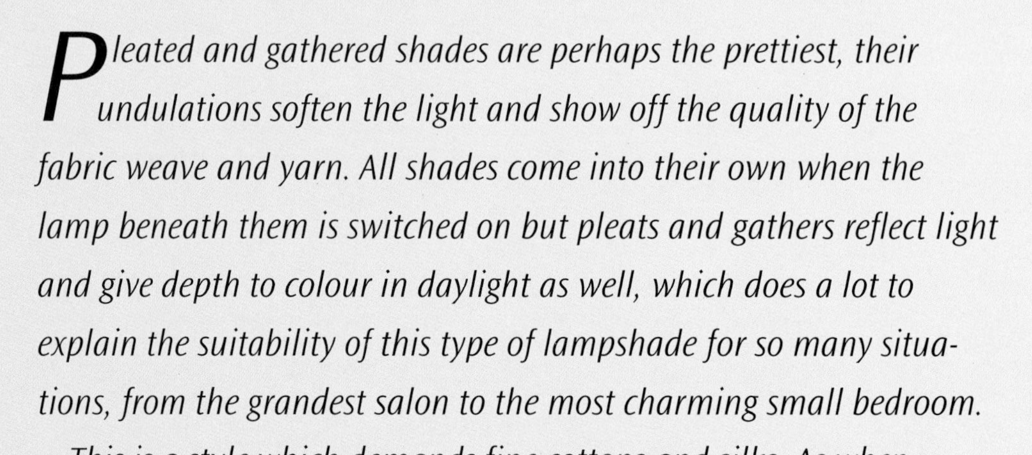

Pleated and gathered shades are perhaps the prettiest, their undulations soften the light and show off the quality of the fabric weave and yarn. All shades come into their own when the lamp beneath them is switched on but pleats and gathers reflect light and give depth to colour in daylight as well, which does a lot to explain the suitability of this type of lampshade for so many situations, from the grandest salon to the most charming small bedroom.

This is a style which demands fine cottons and silks. As when choosing fabric for clothing or other soft furnishings, no decision should be made without gathering up and draping a quantity in order to study the effect of the hidden colour and texture which come to life as the fabric moves. A lamp may be officially redundant in daylight but the curves of gathered cream silk exude warmth and give life to it as an ornament at any time of day.

Here a gathered silk lampshade does justice to another oriental base. Chinese ceramic bases, whether highly glazed and pierced or painted with traditional scenes in blue and white, have been prized for as long as East and West have been trading. Antique bases are no longer allowed out of China but very realistic "aged" versions are being made in Macau for worldwide distribution.

Plain fabrics are an obvious choice for this method, but all manner of checks and stripes, tonal and geometric prints can be very successfully pleated and gathered. Just test a small piece to make sure it works, some prints will simply appear squashed when pleated. Shades can be given a finishing touch with contrasting fabrics - or there is endless opportunity for fun with trimmings: fringes, fan edgings, cords, frills, beads, ribbons, braids, shells, buttons or anything you can dig from the

depths of a cluttered workbox! For this frame the fabric is pleated to the base ring and gathered to the top but variations allow for pleating to both top and base or gathering to both.

Silks and fine cotton chintzes in neutral colours of oyster, cream, buttermilk or sand are universally popular, partly because they are so adaptable to changing situations but mainly because they throw such a lovely warm light in the evenings.

YOU WILL NEED

- *prepared frame (see page 122)*
- *top fabric as chart*
- *lining as chart*
- *matching thread*
- *marking thread*
- *fabric for self-binding or fringe or trimming, as required*

MEASURE

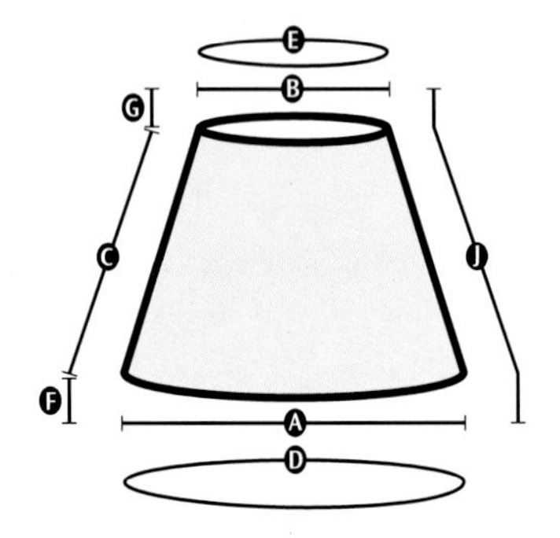

C = slope
D = base circumference
E = top circumference

As a general rule, allow enough fabric to fit two and a half to three times round the top. If your fabric is not wide enough, there is no need to join, as seams would be too bulky and the raw edges are invisibly incorporated into the pleats, but allow for seams on each section. However, if the shade has quite an exaggerated slope, then the pleats should overlap slightly along the top so that they are not too stretched round the base: up to four times the top ring can be used. Allow for self-binding the top and base if required.

Pleated and gathered empire

To make up

1 Cut out the top fabric, lining and self-binding, if using. Place one of the top fabric pieces on the worktable and press.

2 Mark the bottom edge into 3 cm (1¼ in) sections first with pins to establish the spacing, then with a light pencil - leave a space at the end of each strip for joining. Divide the complete width of fabric into the same number of sections as the number of struts in the frame and mark with coloured tacks at top and bottom. (For example, if the fabric is 90 cm/36 in wide to cover three struts, each section will measure 30 cm/12 in.)

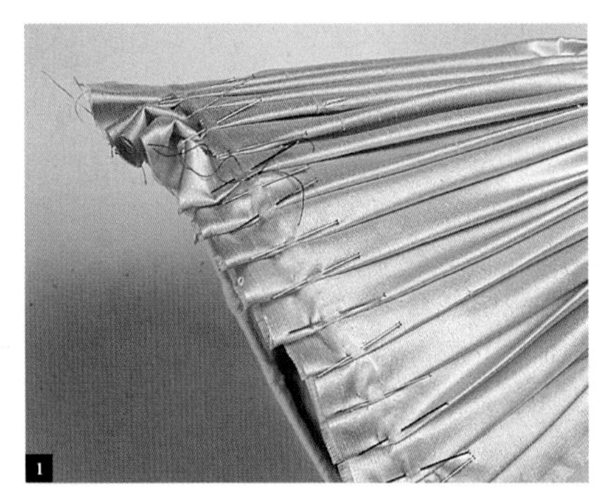
1

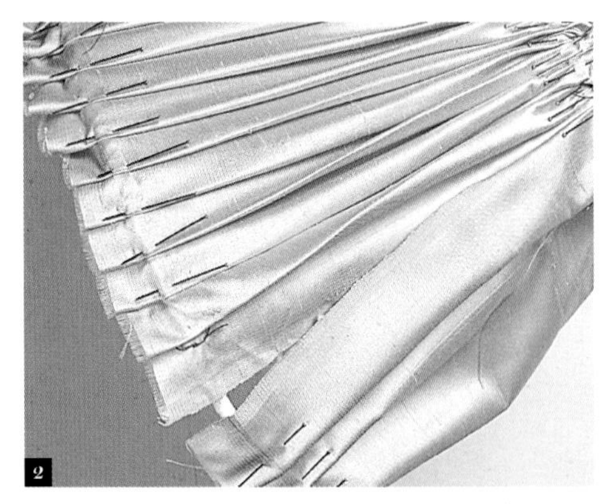
2

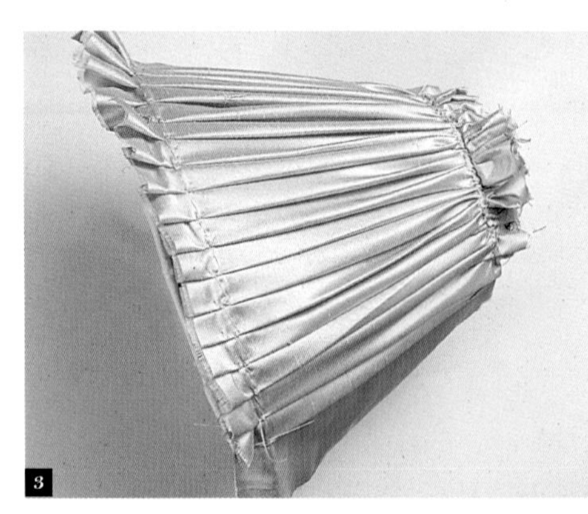
3

3 Take one piece of fabric and pin the first marking tack at the bottom to the base of one of the struts. Pin pleats round the base of the frame, folding each over, so that they start and finish against an adjacent pleat, without overlapping (1).

4 To join the next piece, trim away any selvedge and tuck under the last pleat (2). Cut away any excess, so that the pleats run without interruption. Stitch each pleat to the ring securely, using lampshade stitches 1 - 1.5 cm (⅜ - ⅝ in) in length.

5 For a large frame, run a gathering thread through the fabric level with the top of frame. Pull up slightly and pin each marking tack to a strut. Pull up fully to fit the frame. For a smaller shade, you can just make little tucks at the top. Pin at 1 cm (⅜ in) intervals to hold (2), and stitch down securely to the top ring (3).

6 Make up and fit a tight or pleated lining (see page 122).

7 Self-bind the top and bottom to cover the raw edges (see page 125) or apply fringe or trimming.

Variations

- The hemline may also be gathered, especially on a coolie shade which because of the acute angle is more difficult to pleat satisfactorily. Divide the fabric into the same number of sections as the frame and mark with coloured tacks top and bottom. Pin each marking tack to a frame strut and gather evenly between.
- Both top and base can be pleated. Pleat up the fabric before putting it onto the frame. Pin the bottom edge to the frame. Pull each pleat to the top, overlapping as necessary to keep them running straight. Pin and leave overnight before stitching.

Pleated and gathered shades (above left) can take a variety of edgings, as shown on page 31. Half shades (above right) are effective in dark areas as they allow diffused light through the shade and direct light onto the wall behind. This shade is gathered at top and base.

Re-pin if there has been any sagging (4).
• Tiny 0.25 - 0.5 cm (⅛ - ¼ in) pleats are very effective but time consuming. Choose silk which is very fine and tack each pleat in place before fitting to the frame.

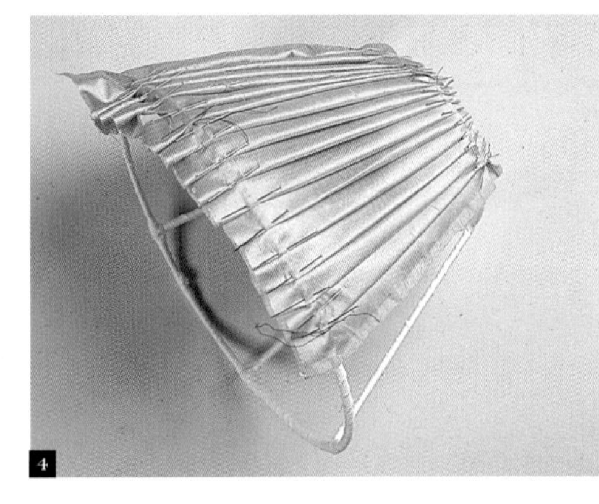

COOLIE *(inches)*

frame size A x B x C	*fabric (2.5 x fullness) width x depth*	*Self binding/braid* top + base*
8 x 3 x 5	64 x 6½	37
10 x 4 x 6	80 x 7½	48
12 x 4 x 7	96 x 8½	54
14 x 4½ x 8	112 x 9½	62
16 x 5 x 9	128 x10½	70
18 x 6 x 10	144 x11½	80
20 x 6 x 11	159 x12½	84

PEMKBROKE *(inches)*

frame size A x B x C	*fabric (3 x fullness) width x depth*	*self binding/braid* top + base*
8 x 4 x 6	78 x 7½	40
10 x 5 x 7	96 x 8½	59
12 x 6 x 8	115 x 9½	60
14 x 7 x 9	134 x 10½	69
16 x 8 x 10	154 x 11½	79
18 x 10 x 12	172 x 13½	94
20 x 11 x 13	190 x 14½	102
22 x 12 x 14	210 x 15½	111

STANDARD EMPIRE *(inches)*

frame size A x B x C	*fabric (3 x fullness) width x depth*	*self binding/braid* top + base*
8 x 5 x 6	80 x 7½	42
10 x 6 x 7	98 x 8½	52
12 x 7 x 8½	116 x 10	60
14 x 9 x 10	134 x 11½	74
16 x 10 x 12	155 x 13½	84
18 x 12 x 14	173 x 15½	95
20 x 13 x 15	190 x 16½	104
22 x 14 x 16	210 x 17½	114

** self-binding should be cut on the cross*

COOLIE *(centimetres)*

frame size A x B x C	*fabric (2.5 x fullness) width x depth*	*Self binding/braid* top + base*
20 x 7.5 x 12.5	163 x 16.5	94
25 x 10 x 15	203 x 19	122
30 x 10 x 18	244 x 21.5	137
35.5 x 11.5 x 20	285 x 24	158
40 x 12.5 x 23	325 x 26.5	178
45.5 x 15 x 25	366 x 29	203
51 x 15 x 28	404 x 32	214

PEMKBROKE *(centimetres)*

frame size A x B x C	*fabric (3 x fullness) width x depth*	*self binding/braid* top + base*
20 x 10 x 15	198 x 19	102
25 x 12.5 x 18	244 x 21.5	150
30 x 15 x 20	292 x 24	153
35.5 x 18 x 23	340 x 26.5	175
40 x 20 x 25	391 x 29	201
45.5 x 25 x 30	437 x 34	239
51 x 28 x 33	483 x 37	259
56 x 30 x 35.5	534 x 39.5	282

STANDARD EMPIRE *(centimetres)*

frame size A x B x C	*fabric (3 x fullness) width x depth*	*self binding/braid* top + base*
20 x 12.5 x 15	203 x 19	107
25 x 15 x 18	249 x 21.5	132
30 x 18 x 21.5	295 x 25	153
35.5 x 23 x 25	340 x 29	188
40 x 25 x 30	394 x 34	214
45.5 x 30 x 35.5	440 x 39.5	241
51 x 33 x 38	483 x 42	264
56 x 35.5 x 40	534 x 44.5	290

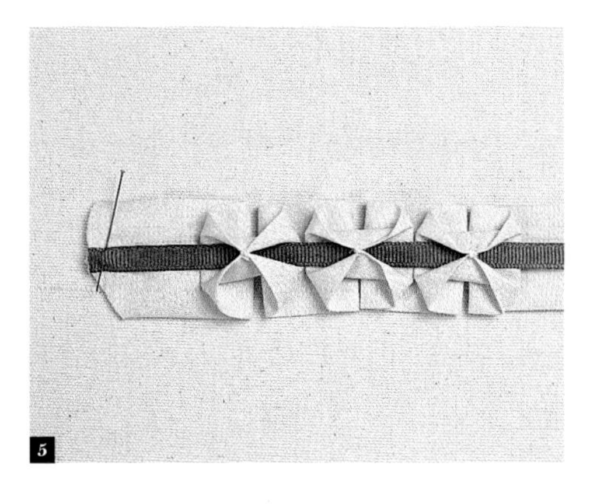

Butterfly edging

Cut strips of fabric two and two-thirds times the size of the finished edging. In this case 16 cm (6½ in) for a 6 cm (2½ in) frill. Join strips to make three times the circumference in length. Press 6 cm (2½ in) to the wrong side lengthwise, then the remaining 4 cm (1½ in) to the back. Pleat into box pleats as wide as the depth of the folded strip (in this case 6 cm/2½ in). Stitch through the centre by hand or using a machine. Take the centre top and bottom of each pleat and stitch together with matching thread to be invisible or with embroidery cotton for a detail. Thread velvet ribbon through to cover the stitching line (5).

This frame (right) has been pleated at top and base as described in the variations to the main method on page 28. Deep fringing is always elegant, especially when it is made of linen or silk to tone with the main shade fabric. At the top of the frame, which has been self-bound, chunky wool pom pom tassels offer a light-hearted touch.

A

B

C

D

E

F

Edgings gallery

A Self-bound edges are neat, classical and often all that is needed but there are so many lovely trimmings that you might prefer to add some detail either immediately or in several years' time when the binding is looking a little tired. A twisted cord chosen to match drapes, cushions, lamp base or even wallcovering can be stitched close to the top of a self-bound edge.

B Any pretty fan edging in place of a bound edge will add interest to a shade and this handmade edging with its wooden "olives", copied from an ancient French design is, I think, particularly charming.

C Frills made from the same fabric as the shade introduce a feminine touch. Cut a length of fabric two and a half times the circumference in length and 10 cm (4 in) wide. With right sides facing, stitch the two long sides together to make a tube. Turn right side out and press, so that the seam falls 1.5 cm (⅝ in) down from the top edge. Neaten the two short ends by hand and either stitch together or overlap. Gather to fit. Hand stitch to the frame along the gathering line.

D Make a self frill as described above, then stitch a narrow cord or twisted braid on top covering the stitching line.

E Handmade fringing is luxurious with ice cream tassels.

F Two-toned cut fringing gives a delicate, elegant finish. Comb the fringe or hold carefully over steam if it starts to curl.

Twisted roll

This box-pleated shade is decorated with twisted lengths of fabric at the bottom and top of the frame. Choose fabric with a good texture and body - here rich velvet complements the deep red habutai silk. Each of these rolls was cut 16 cm (6½ in) wide and double the circumference, the lower roll has been twisted more lightly than the top roll. Tuck raw edges out of sight and slipstitch to hold in place.

One-piece shade

It is possible to make a pleated and/or gathered shade incorporating top and bottom frills with just a single strip of fabric. Cut the fabric to twice the base circumference in length and 12 cm (4¾ in) deeper than the frame. Adjust the depth for a different sized frame. Seam the short sides together. Make rolled hems at the top and bottom and shell stitch as shown on page 124. Run gathering threads through, 6 cm (2½ in) from the hem and 3 cm (1¼ in) from the heading. Fit either a pleated or tight lining to the frame following instructions on page 122.

Divide the shade fabric into sections equal to the number of struts in your frame and mark each division with a coloured tack on both top and bottom gathering lines.

Starting at the top of the frame, pin each tack to the top ring level with a strut join. Gather up each section evenly and pin at 1 cm (⅜ in) intervals. Stitch in place using lampshade stitches, then pin the fabric to the base ring, pulling the fabric taut as you go. Gather up as before. Leave overnight and re-pin if the pleats have sagged at all. Stitch to the frame. Cover the stitching lines at top and base with gimp, double fan-edged braid or fabric binding.

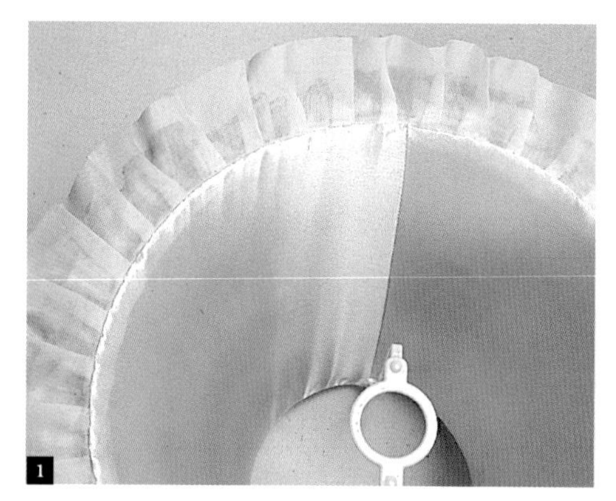

Double frilled hem

Hand-woven silk with a cotton organdie lower frill are a winning and ethereal combination. English silk, French Toile de Jouy cupboard curtains, an Indian painted lampbase, a Chinese bowl and lacquered clock case perfectly prove the success of mixing eastern and western traditions.

Make up the pleated and/or gathered shade following the method on pages 28-9 and bind the top as shown on page 125.

Cut two strips of fabric, both three times the base circumference in length and double the width of the finished frill, plus an allowance for the seams. The top frill should be a little shorter than the under frill. Fold in half, right sides together, and seam lengthwise. Turn right side out. Press, and join the short sides together by hand. Gather up and stitch the under frill to the inside bottom edge of the frame (1).

For the top frill, machine one row of stitching on the fold line and another 1 cm (3/8 in) inside. Run two gathering threads along the same lines. Pull up and pin evenly to the frame. Stitch to the shade fabric with tiny stitches to prevent gaping between the folds (2). Remove the gathering threads.

It's always fun to add checks to traditional floral chintz designs. Here (left) tiny checked taffeta has been used on the straight for the frill and cut on the cross as a perfect binding for the top edge.

Card Shades

These shades provide a good base on which to display boldly patterned fabrics.

Card shades can be put together quickly and used as under shades for the ideas featured later in this book or they can be covered in fabric and star in their own right. Any fabric which is tightly and evenly woven can be used: 100% natural fabrics, in particular cotton and linen, are the easiest to work with, as they press crisply, handle well and adhere to the backing reliably. The basic shade can also be covered in paper: wallpaper, wrapping paper, heavyweight tissues, book binding and other handmade papers are just a few of the alternatives to fabric, all made up using exactly the same method.

Pleated fabric-on-card shades are attractive on candle lamps, side and wall lamps and useful as shades for ceiling lights in areas which often present problems, such as children's rooms, guest bedrooms and bathrooms.

Choose designs of a suitable scale and character: ginghams, small checks and Provençal prints make delightful candle shades for kitchen table suppers, larger checks and plaids complement pretty chintzes or heavy weaves, flowers and unbleached linen look good next to crisp, white bedlinen. Some shades may blend into the surroundings, others may become main features. A complete fake fur room is a rarity but one or two leopard skin shades can provide a chic surprise set in sophisticated white and grey surroundings or among richly coloured fabrics and furnishings.

It is worth bearing in mind that the card inside the shade can also be coloured: either paint it yourself or use pre-coloured card - perhaps a primary colour for a child's room or gold for a study. The more adventurous can paint or stencil motifs, checks or stripes on the inner card before making up and edges can be cut into scallops, pinked, bound, painted or threaded with ribbon to finish off.

There are templates for three sizes of fabric-covered card shades, but also fabric quantities for larger shades, as you may wish to re-cover an existing shade or make templates for other sizes. It is possible to cover an old card shade with fabric, but be sure to test a small area first to make sure that the under shade does not react to the new layer of glue. These shades can be

made to any size from the smallest candle shade up to standard lamp dimensions. The top of the shade is fitted with a metal ring which holds the card in a perfect circle and provides the lamp fitting. Smaller shades will only need the top ring but any shade with a base diameter greater than 25 cm (10 in) will need the support of a base ring. The basic card needs to be strong but flexible. Parchment papers in natural and white are available from crafts suppliers. There are also many lovely handmade papers from all over the world, the heaviest of which can be used most satisfactorily; the lightest will need to be glued to a stronger card base.

YOU WILL NEED

- *plain card or self-adhesive backing*
- *fabric to cover card, see chart*
- *masking tape*
- *PVA glue and brush*
- *ruler*
- *clothes' peg or large paper clip*
- *scissors, hole punch or ribbon for decorating the lower edge*
- *top ring with lamp fitting*
- *base ring (depending on size of frame)*
- *point turner or short knitting needle*

This calico-covered card shade with taped edges (above) is the model for the shades used under all of the slipcover shades.

Shade type and size (inches)		*Fabric*	*Ribbon for base trim*
Candle	6 x 2¼ x 4½	14 x 12	2 yds
Coolie	8 x 3 x 5½	14 x 20	2½ yds
Coolie	10 x 3 x 6½	22 x 18	3 yds
Coolie	12 x 4 x 7	24 x 18	3½ yds
Empire	10 x 5 x 7	28 x 22	3½ yds
Empire	12 x 6 x 8	32 x 24	3½ yds
Pembroke	12 x 7 x 8½	36 x 26	3½ yds

All of these shades are used throughout the book and templates are given for four of the sizes on pages 42, 43 and 65.

Shade type and size (centimetres)		*Fabric*	*Ribbon for base trim*
Candle	15 x 5.5 x 11.5	35 x 30	2 m
Coolie	20 x 7.5 x 14	35 x 50	2.20 m
Coolie	25 x 7.5 x 16.5	55 x 45	2.5 m
Coolie	30 x 10 x 18	60 x 45	3 m
Empire	25 x 12.5 x 18	70 x 55	3 m
Empire	30 x 15 x 20	80 x 60	3 m
Pembroke	30 x 18 x 21.5	90 x 65	3 m

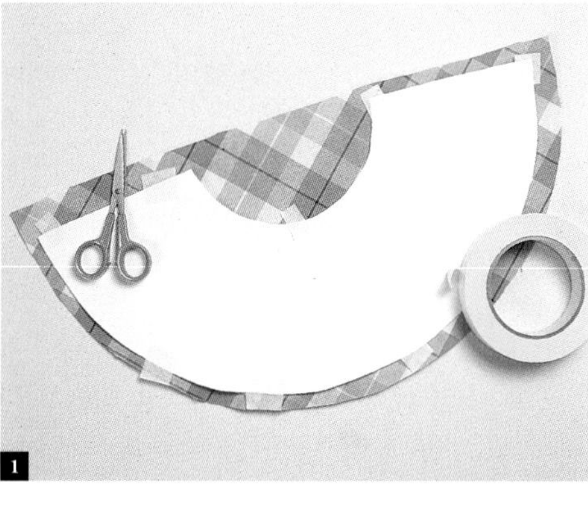

1

2

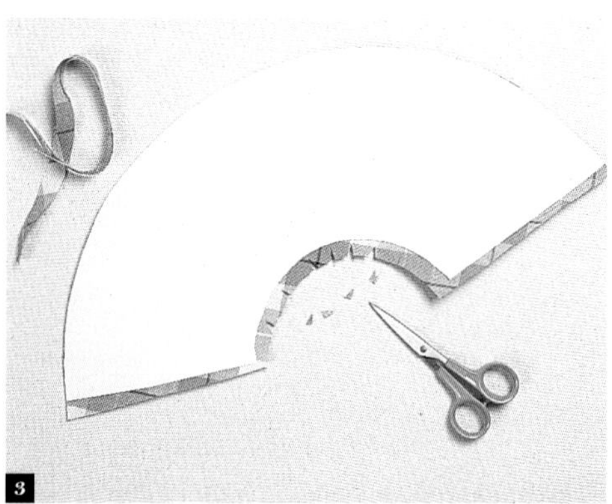

3

4

Fabric-covered card shade

To make up

1 Cut the card or self-adhesive backing using one of the templates given on pages 42-3. Place the fabric on the worktable and press under a damp cloth to remove all creases. Place the card template over the fabric, secure with masking tape and cut the fabric roughly to shape (1).

2 Spread a thin, even layer of glue over the card, or remove the plastic film from the self-adhesive backing. Starting from one short side, roll the fabric over the card (2), smoothing any bubbles away with the flat of the ruler. Leave to dry.

3 If you are just using a top ring, trim the fabric close to the card along the bottom edge and leave 1.5 cm (5/8 in) fabric at the top and sides. If you need to use a base ring as well, trim fabric to 1.5 cm (5/8 in) all round. Snip the fabric at 1 cm (3/8 in) intervals at the top of the shade (3).

4 Decorate the lower edge at this stage if you are going to and if you are not using a base ring, for example, bind, paint, pink or punch holes through the edges (4).

5 Spread a little glue along the short overlap edge. Bring the short edges of the card together, so that they butt up against each other. Press down the overlaps and hold with a clothes' peg or large paper clip at both ends until dry. Glue the fabric lightly on the wrong side and press the ring inside against the card. Fold the fabric over and tuck it under the ring.

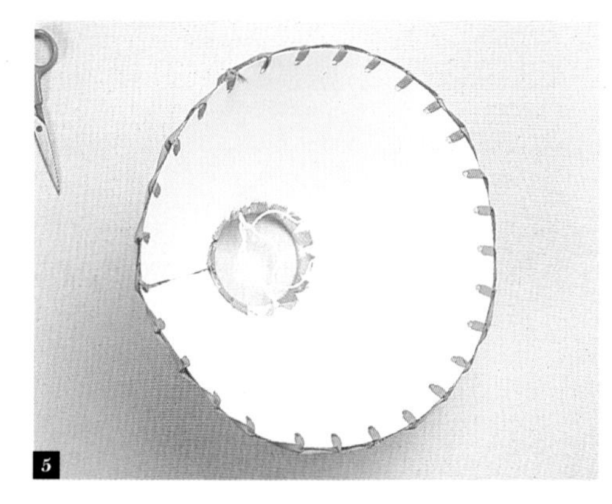

5

6 You will need to snip the fabric away a little round the lamp fitting so that it can lie flat (5). Use a point turner or short knitting needle to roll the edges right under the ring. Repeat for the base ring, if using.

Taped edges

The top and bottom edges can be bound together with sticky tape for an easier finish, particularly if the fabric frays badly. This method is not as neat but perfectly adequate if there are trimmings to add, or if a slipcover will be made to fit over. Any neutral coloured masking or drafting tape can be used.

Cut the fabric tightly against the card along the top and bottom edges. Glue, overlap and secure the short edges until firmly adhered as before. Carefully unroll tape from the reel and stick it evenly to the edge of the shade. Hold the ring inside the shade against the card and secure with small strips of tape. Fold the tape over to enclose the ring, peeling off the small holding strips as you come to them.

Scalloped edges

Scalloped edges are attractive but need to be cut with very sharp scissors to prevent any unsightly frayed threads. You could bind the edge, add ribbon or pink it. Alternatively, you could use a thick felt-tipped pen or a thin brush and paint to add a coloured border round the base to accentuate the scallops.

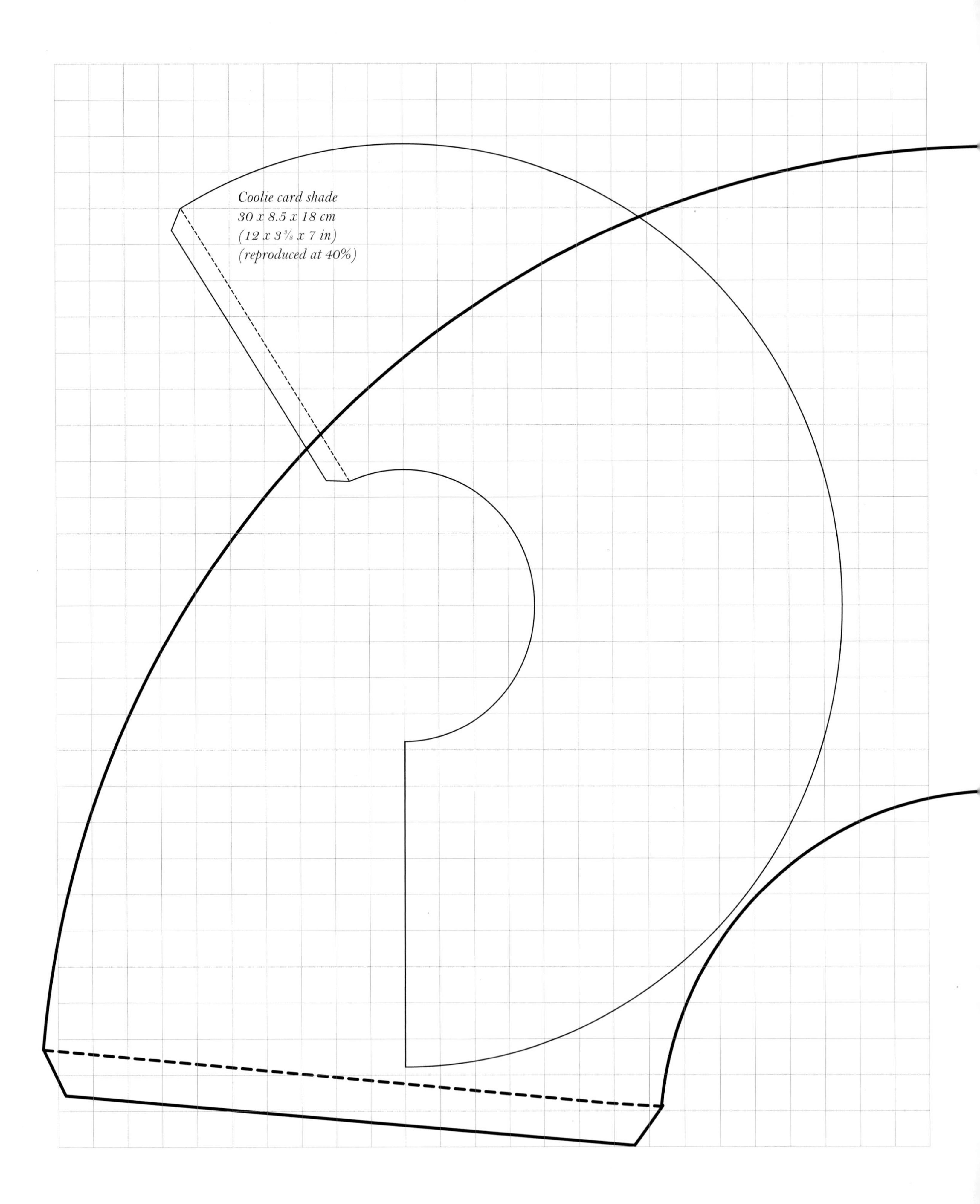

Coolie card shade
30 x 8.5 x 18 cm
(12 x 3⅜ x 7 in)
(reproduced at 40%)

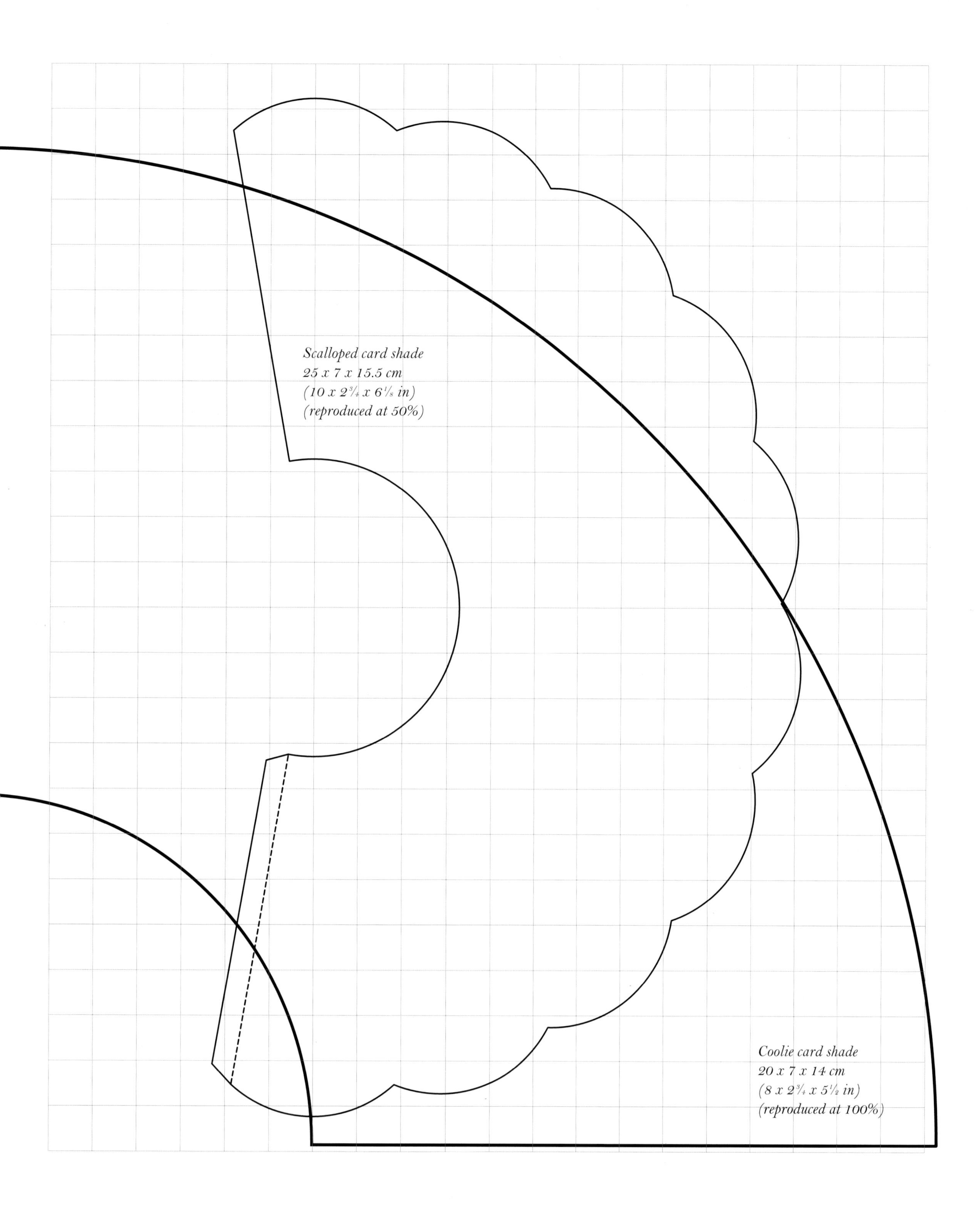
Scalloped card shade
25 x 7 x 15.5 cm
(10 x 2¾ x 6⅛ in)
(reproduced at 50%)
Coolie card shade
20 x 7 x 14 cm
(8 x 2¾ x 5½ in)
(reproduced at 100%)

Square and rectangular shades can be made following the same principles as round shades but the top and bottom "rings" are only available from a specialist source. A small square shade template is given on page 66. To make other sizes, mock them up first using stiff card and sticky tape. The tweed cover photographed (right) has been chosen to fit in a hallway, sitting above the walking stick collection.

Any shape of card shade can be made to suit a new or existing lamp base (far right). Alternatively, if you have an under shade still in good condition, just cover it, making sure that the adhesive you use will not be affected by heat.

SPEED THE
OUGH

YOU WILL NEED

- *plain card or self-adhesive material, see chart*
- *fabric, see chart*
- *PVA glue and brush*
- *ruler and pencil*
- *set square*
- *craft knife*
- *top ring with lamp fitting*
- *base ring (depending on size of frame)*
- *ribbon or paint to decorate rings (optional)*
- *cord for bow (optional)*

PLEATED SHADES *(inches)*

shade size	*fabric width x depth*	*ribbon to wind round ring*
8 x 3 x 5½	72 x 6	2½ yds
9 x 3 x 6	81 x 6½	2½ yds
10 x 3 x 6½	90 x 7	2½ yds
11 x 3½ x 7	99 x 7½	2½ yds
12 x 3½ x 7	108 x 7½	2½ yds
13 x 4 x 7½	120 x 8	3½ yds
14 x 4½ x 8	130 x 8½	3½ yds
15 x 5 x 8½	135 x 9	3½ yds
16 x 5 x 9	145 x 9½	4½ yds
17 x 5 x 9½	155 x 10	4½ yds
18 x 6 x 10	165 x 10½	4½ yds

PLEATED SHADES *(centimetres)*

shade size	*fabric width x depth*	*ribbon to wind round ring*
20 x 7.5 x 14	180 x 15	2 m
23 x 7.5 x 15	200 x 17	2 m
25 x 7.5 x 16.5	220 x 18	2 m
28 x 9 x 18	240 x 20	2 m
30 x 9 x 18	260 x 20	2 m
33 x 10 x 19	300 x 21	3 m
35.5 x 11.5 x 20	320 x 22	3 m
38 x 12.5 x 21.5	335 x 23	3 m
40 x 12.5 x 23	360 25	4 m
43 x 12.5 x 24	390 x 27	4 m
45.5 x 15 x 25	410 x 28	4 m

The self adhesive backing or card should be the exact depth of the finished shade. The width is as for fabric

Pleated shade

Small pleated shades are substantial enough with just a top ring but larger shades will benefit from an additional ring near the bottom or from being fitted to a full frame. However, if the shade is to be hung from the ceiling, use rings as the frame will look ugly. Either paint the rings to match the fabric or weave ribbon round the ring before you fit the shade. A bow made from cord in a matching colour can be stitched to the completed shade if liked.

Suitable materials

This shade is made with fabric and card but pleated shades can also be made with paper-covered card. Lightweight papers will need to be glued to a card backing but many are heavy enough to hold the pleating. Any tightly and evenly woven fabrics can be used and almost any print - even really large designs can look most effective when pleated up.

To make up

1 Cut the card and fabric to the size chosen from the chart. Press the fabric flat to remove any creases. If using plain card, paste a thin even layer of glue over half the card, starting at one short side. If using self-adhesive material, peel back half of the film, with the sticky side towards the fabric, carefully lining up the long sides (1). Take care not to stretch the fabric and smooth out any bubbles. Glue or unpeel the other side. Smooth down and leave to dry. Trim away any excess fabric leaving 1.5 cm (⅝ in) along each short side.

2 With the ruler and pencil, mark the pleat sizes on the card side, along the long sides, top and bottom. Use a set square to check that the lines are at right angles to the long sides.

3 Make the pleats, folding each along the length of the ruler, concertina style. Score along the pencilled lines first if the pleats are not folding sharply (2).

1

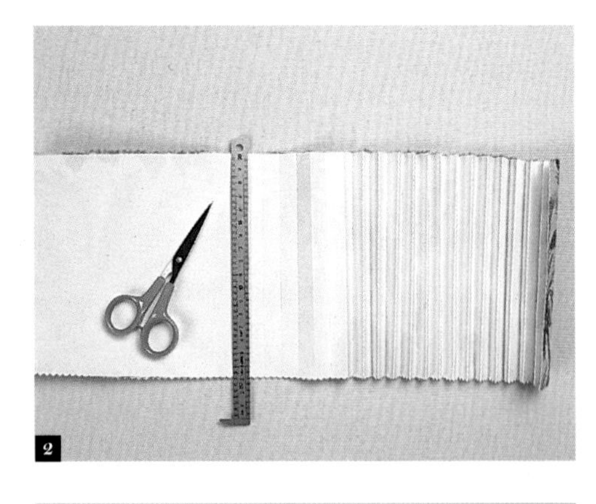
2

3

4

4 Cut out notches at the back of each pleat approximately 2.5 cm (1 in) from the top. To do this, transfer the shape given in the diagram opposite and use a sharp knife to work neatly (3). If using a lower ring, measure carefully and make notches at a uniform distance from the bottom edge. Paint or bind the rings, if liked.

5 Spread a thin layer of glue along the short sides. Bring the short sides together, overlapping the fabric and butting up the card. Hold in place at either end. When quite dry, slip the shade over the ring or rings, pressing each notch firmly into position (4). Neaten the bottom edge at the join if necessary.

actual size of notch to cut

Pinpricked and Pierced Shades

I have to confess that I stencilled this design onto a bought calico shade. I chose to stencil in just three colours - apricot, green and yellow, with the yellow used as a highlight colour for the others, as I wanted the relief to be the focal point, rather than a riot of colours.

As the previous chapter shows, card shades are simple to make at home and provide endless creative possibilities. Here, we take the basic method one stage further and let the light play through holes cut in the shade, providing interesting effects when the lamp is switched on and an eye-catching feature when the lamp is off.

Flower petals cut in relief on stencilled shades uncurl to reveal a glow of colour - not only is a design given life with a step into the third dimension but also a coloured card lining reflects and filters, producing deeper tones and contrast colours. Try using tissue as a lining, it will transform the colour of a plain bulb. Or on fabric-covered card shades cut away part of the fabric design, to give the texture of a relief and allow the light to glow through varying depths.

Step back into childhood and play dot-to-dot by piercing holes along the outline of a design, combine this with relief cutting or ring the changes with coloured linings. These shades need not match your furnishing fabrics too slavishly, you can mimic a motif found anywhere in the room or pick up a general theme: fruit and flowers, seascapes and waves... As the materials are not expensive you can afford to experiment with light and form to your heart's content.

YOU WILL NEED

- *gold, silver or coloured card*
- *fabric, see chart on page 40*
- *cutting board*
- *craft knife*
- *masking tape*
- *PVA glue and brush*
- *top and base rings*
- *point turner or short knitting needle*
- *clothes' peg or large paper clip*

Patterned fabric shade

You can make these fabric-covered card shades using only household tools: needles of various sizes, a steel ruler, craft knife, hole punch and cutting board. If you don't have a good cutting board, a piece of thick card or a piece of glass or wood will suffice - these will all just blunt your knife a little more quickly. Keep masking tape and a tub of glue on hand in case of error. Think about using gold, silver or coloured card for the inside. Once the shapes are cut, the colour will just be seen and will throw an interesting light through the holes.

Suitable fabrics

Choose tightly woven cottons, which will not fray and which have motifs suitable for cutting and piercing. Stylised motifs should be cut evenly, while rambling designs may be varied and cut randomly.

To make up

1 Make up a basic shade covered with fabric as shown on page 41, but don't position the rings or close the sides.

2 Place the shade onto the cutting surface. Decide which and how many of the motifs in the fabric you wish to cut and

raise off the shade. Using a craft knife, cut carefully, lifting the cut section with the edge of the knife to see how much more needs to be cut. Each piece should stay firm but be able to sit slightly proud and each should be facing the same direction - think of the way shadows fall. Never cut more than two-thirds to three-quarters of any shape or the section will drop out and all you will have is an ugly hole!

3 Finish making the shade following the instructions on page 41.

Card variation

The stencil template below (photographed on page 49) will fit a card coolie shade 40 x 11.5 x 23 cm (16 x 4½ x 9 in) but may be adapted to other sizes by adjusting the design a little or by photocopying it to a different scale.

To make your own design, wrap stencil acetate or tracing paper round the made-up shade, making sure it fits snugly. Anchor in place with masking tape and pins pushed through above the top ring and below the bottom ring to avoid pinning through the shade. Carefully pencil round the top and bottom edges and along the join. Cut to shape and draw or trace your own design onto the matt side.

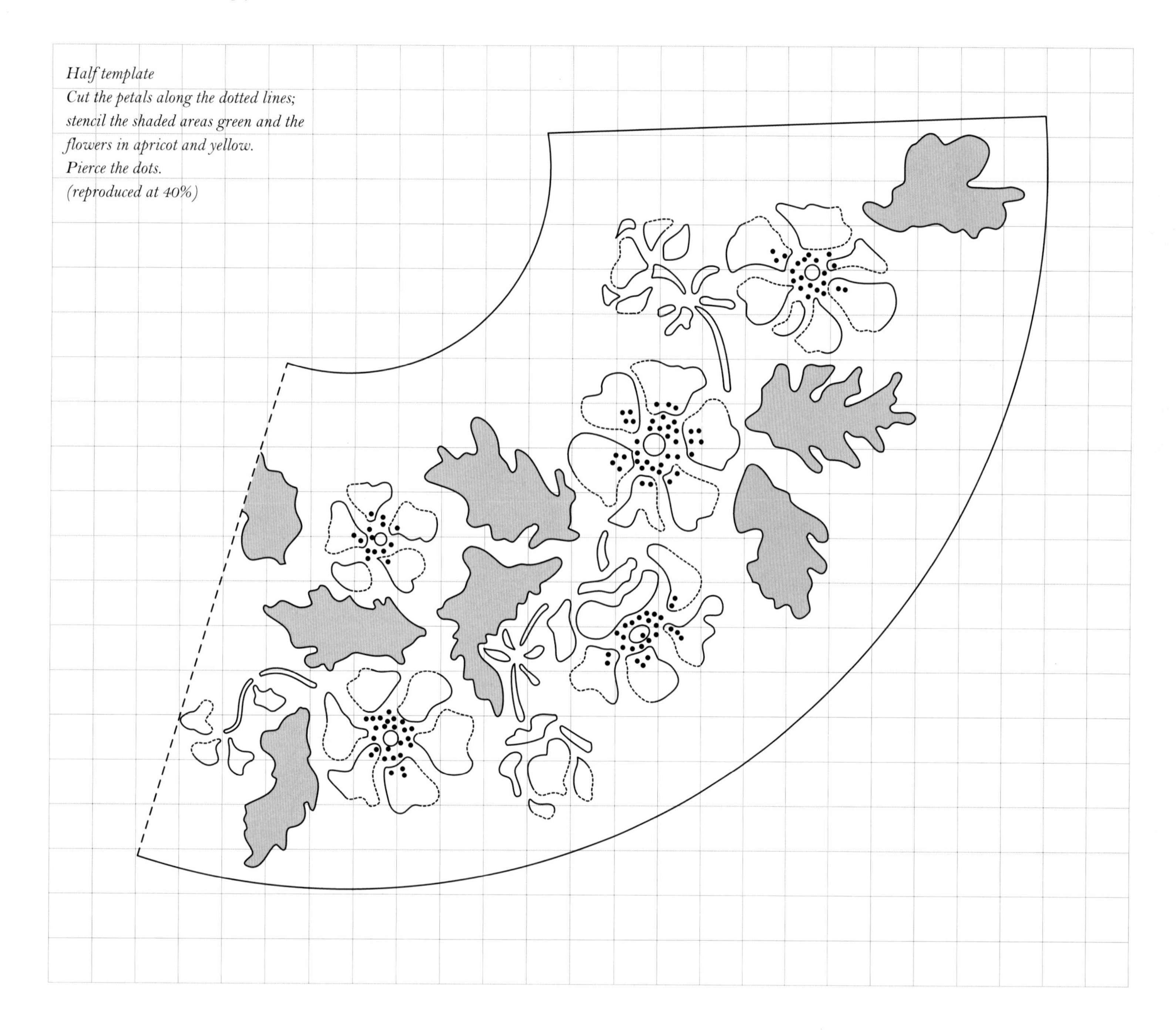

Half template
Cut the petals along the dotted lines; stencil the shaded areas green and the flowers in apricot and yellow.
Pierce the dots.
(reproduced at 40%)

YOU WILL NEED

- *medium weight card*
- *stencil acetate or tracing paper*
- *craft knife*
- *cutting board*
- *darning needle or knitting needle*
- *tissue*
- *PVA glue and brush*
- *5 cm (2 in) candle bulb shade fitting*

Oak leaf and acorn shade

Design your own simple motif to reflect a theme or fabric in your furnishings. The design used here looks to the countryside for its inspiration.

To make up

1 Cut your card template using the shape below. Place onto a sheet of stencil acetate or tracing paper and cut out. Trace the design below onto the matt side of the acetate or onto the tracing paper. Place the shade onto the cutting surface, front side down and transfer the design onto the back.

Note: *If you are using your own design, always position it with the centre just below the centre of the shade. If set too high, it will appear to be floating off into the air.*

2 Using the craft knife and darning needle, pierce and cut through the card as marked.

3 When the design has been fully cut out, gently bend each piece back with your fingers, so that the sides just roll slightly. This will give you neat, sculpted cuts instead of hard edges. From the front check that each piece is neatly finished.

4 Cut the tissue for the lining using the shade template. Trim away just 2 mm (1/12 in) away all round. Paste a line of glue on the inside of the shade, all round the edges. Lay the tissue lightly over. Press onto the glue, smoothing out any wrinkles and hold until firm.

5 Glue the short edges together and hold in place until firm. Add any further decoration or binding once the shade is quite dry. Place the shade over the candle fitting.

Child's Play

These simple throwover shades are so quick to make that you can use them as temporary or as seasonal covers.

The theory that small children become relaxed in multi-coloured rooms has certainly influenced the design of children's toys and furnishing fabrics in the last two decades. Indeed, if you invite children to choose their own furnishings, they will almost always head straight for the vibrant primaries.

Practical fabrics, such as denim, felt and gingham, and checks, stripes and simple ethnic prints, all mix well with typical children's clutter and readily accept simple decoration. So there is no need to hunt for nursery lampshades - throwover squares are quick to make and can easily be changed as your child grows up. They can disguise an ugly shade or just be used as a temporary measure while you are settling into a new house.

Even very young children enjoy helping to make a felt shade cover for their bedroom. Such covers can be popped over a shade at night to provide a subdued light, dense felt lets just enough light out to comfort a toddler or allow you to feed a baby. A shoe lace threaded through holes punched in the fabric can be adjusted to fit varying shade sizes and children will love to help you choose buttons for decoration - a visit to a specialist shop will reveal a myriad of teddies, pandas, stars, bees and, of course, ladybirds.

Hems can be finished neatly and quickly: fold under the raw edge and blanket stitch with wool or embroidery thread, or stitch ribbon, cord, ric-rac braid or other trimmings over the raw edges. Cut appliqué designs from felt or other non-fraying fabrics to save time on neatening the edges.

These slipcover shades can be used for table lamps or for ceiling lights and any kind of fabric can be used, patterned or plain as shown here, in a colour either to let the light through or to dim it for night-time use.

YOU WILL NEED

- *card or fabric under shade*
- *top fabric square, see below*
- *wool, ribbon, braid, pom poms or shells, to decorate*
- *pair of compasses or small ruler*
- *for the bee appliqué: yellow, black and white felt*
- *PVA glue and brush or matching threads*
- *black felt-tipped pen*

MEASURE

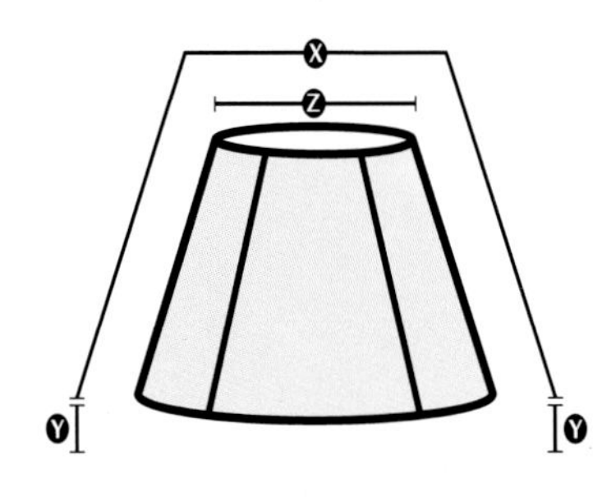

X = up one side, straight across the top ring and down the other
Y = suitable over-hang
Z = top diameter

These shades are made from a fabric square, which needs to be large enough to completely cover the under shade but not so huge that it just hangs limply. So, for a small sidelight shade, add just 3 cm (1¼ in) plus 2 cm (¾ in) seam allowance to measurement X and 6 -7 cm (2½ - 2¾ in) extra plus seam allowance for a large ceiling shade. Felt needs no seam allowance as it cuts cleanly.

Square throwover with bee appliqué

Simple motifs to decorate the fabric squares are easy to design, cut and appliqué. Take inspiration from children's books, birthday cards and craft magazines. Stitch in place by hand with blanket stitch or by machine with satin stitch.

Suitable fabrics

Felt or a non-fraying fabric are best for the appliqué, the square can be cotton or a light wool.

To make up

1 Cut out the fabric square, turn under 2cm (¾ in), then finish the edges with blanket stitch or turn to the right side and finish with ribbon or braid (see page 123).

2 To mark the centre hole, fold the square into a quarter. Use a pair of compasses or a small ruler and pin the radius measurement. Move the pins inwards to make a smaller hole, taking into account the seam allowance you will need. Cut out the centre circle. Snip into the seam allowance to allow it to be turned, then finish the edge with ribbon, braid or blanket stitch as for the edges.

3 To appliqué the bee motif, cut out the main body (A) and face (B) from yellow felt. From black felt, cut the wings (C, D), stripes (E, F) and eyes (G). Use white felt or cotton for the other eye pieces (H). Glue or stitch the stripes to the body of the bee. Make the face with the felt eyes and a felt-tipped mouth. Assemble the bee in one corner of the shade cover. Secure with pins, then glue or stitch in place.

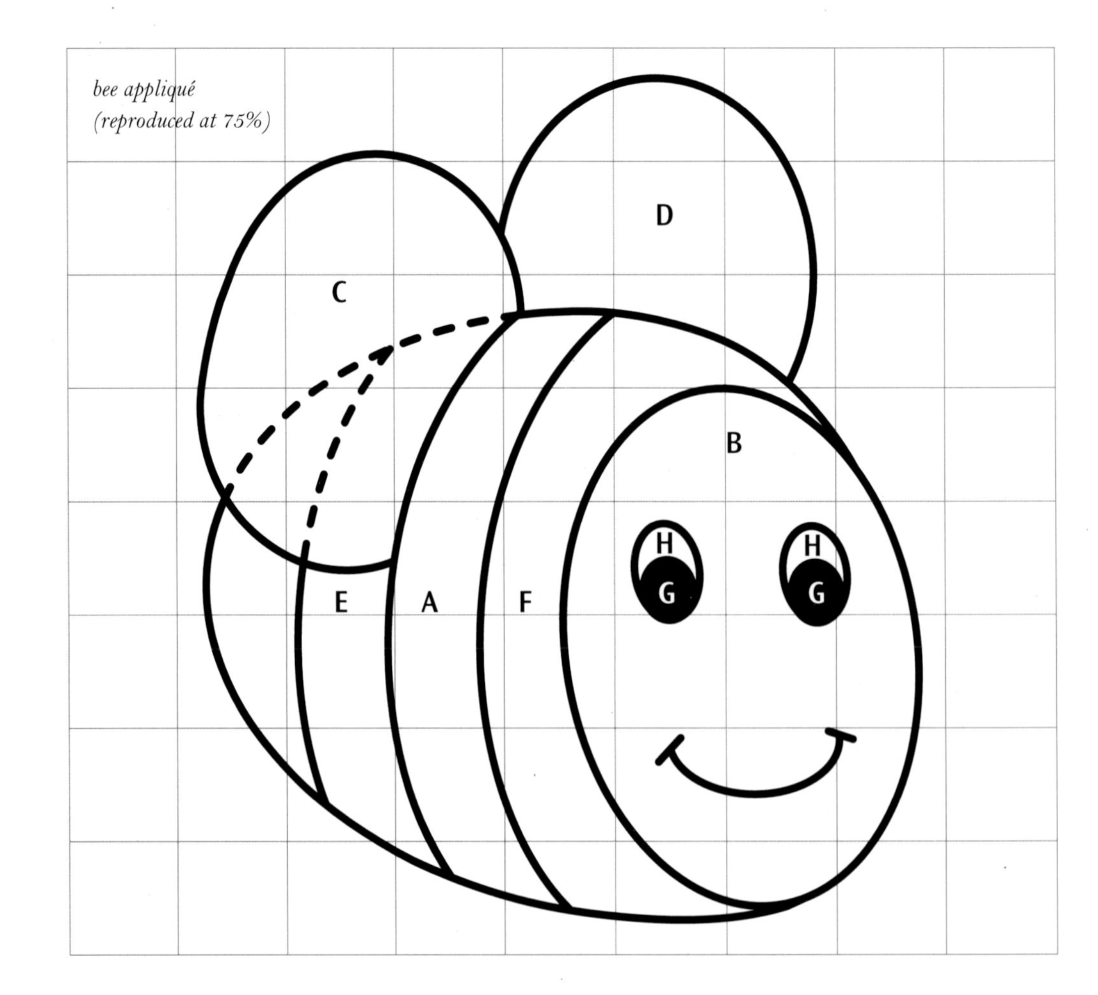

Milestones

Simple card shades for candles are quick to make to decorate any celebration.

The possibilities for decorating card shades are limited only by your imagination. It is so easy to produce a plain card shade and to embellish it, that this is an ideal way to provide celebratory lighting for a special occasion. Candle shades are particularly suitable for this type of project and will add an eye-catching personal touch to side tables and mantlepieces or as the centrepiece of a table set for a festive meal.

These shades are the equivalent of homemade greetings cards -they don't have to be perfect, what is most important is the thought that has gone into them - they will be appreciated much more than any number of shop-bought decorations. You can use the templates given in this book or use worn out junk shop finds as templates, look out for unusual shapes and sizes. Any card which will bend into a tube without cracking or without being too limp can be used.

Decoration can be as simple or as elaborate as time and inspiration will allow. Don't worry if you are not feeling particularly artistic, you can always look for ideas in other sources, such as children's books, old birthday and Christmas cards or magazines. These shades should be cheerful and spontaneous, so don't labour over them.

Remember not to leave a candle burning in an unoccupied room.

MON·DROIT
QUARRY HILL
ITALY, 1943-45
MEDENINE
ANZIO

50

YOU WILL NEED

- *felt-tipped film writing pen*
- *acetate stencil film*
- *craft knife*
- *cutting board (self-healing if available)*
- *250 gsm card*
- *masking tape*
- *steel ruler*
- *stencil paints*
- *stencil brushes*
- *PVA glue and brush*
- *candle fitting*

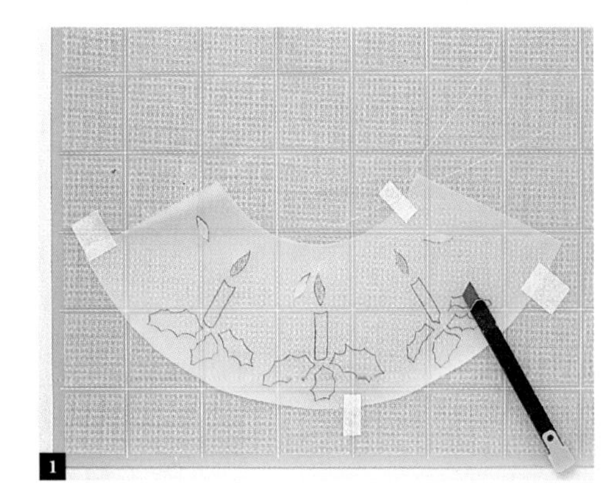

Christmas candle shade

This quickly made card shade has a stencilled design on a Christmas theme, however, the principle can be applied to any other special occasion, using an appropriate motif, as shown on the previous two pages. Templates are given on pages 66-7. The shades are designed to sit on top of a candle fitting.

To make up

1 Using the felt-tipped pen, draw the template for the shape of the shade (see page 65) straight onto the acetate film.

2 Cut out the shape from the film, using the sharp craft knife and working on the cutting board (1). If possible, use a self-healing board, otherwise use a piece of thick card or wood. This will blunt the knife a bit more quickly but it's cheaper than buying a board if you only want to make a few shades.

3 Place the acetate template onto the card, hold it down with masking tape and draw round it (2). If you're righthanded, keep your left hand on the card and cut in long sweeps. If you are lefthanded, use your right hand to steady the card. Use a steel ruler to guide the knife along the straight edges. Turn the board and card as necessary, don't try to cut round the card without moving it or you will obscure your vision and will be more likely to make a mistake.

4 Space the shapes or patterns evenly on the card. You should be able to fit three or four shapes on each shade. Make

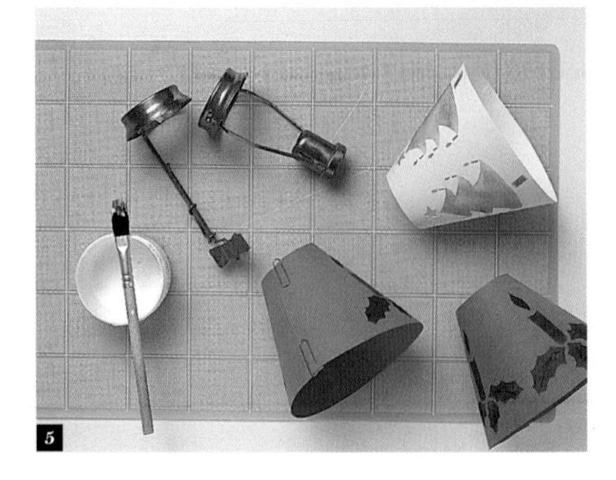

any cut-out shapes using a continuous sweep of the knife. Apply the decoration or paint on the stencils, depending which decorative method you are using (3). Whichever method you use, don't worry too much if the holly leaf, or whatever, isn't a perfect shape, these are spontaneous, single occasion shades (4).

5 Using a small brush, apply a thin line of glue along the edge of the card as indicated on the template. When tacky, overlap the two straight edges, press together and hold firmly with paper clips until stuck fast (5), then slip over the candle fitting.

Alternative motif for the Christmas candle shade, cut the shaded area (reproduced at 100%)

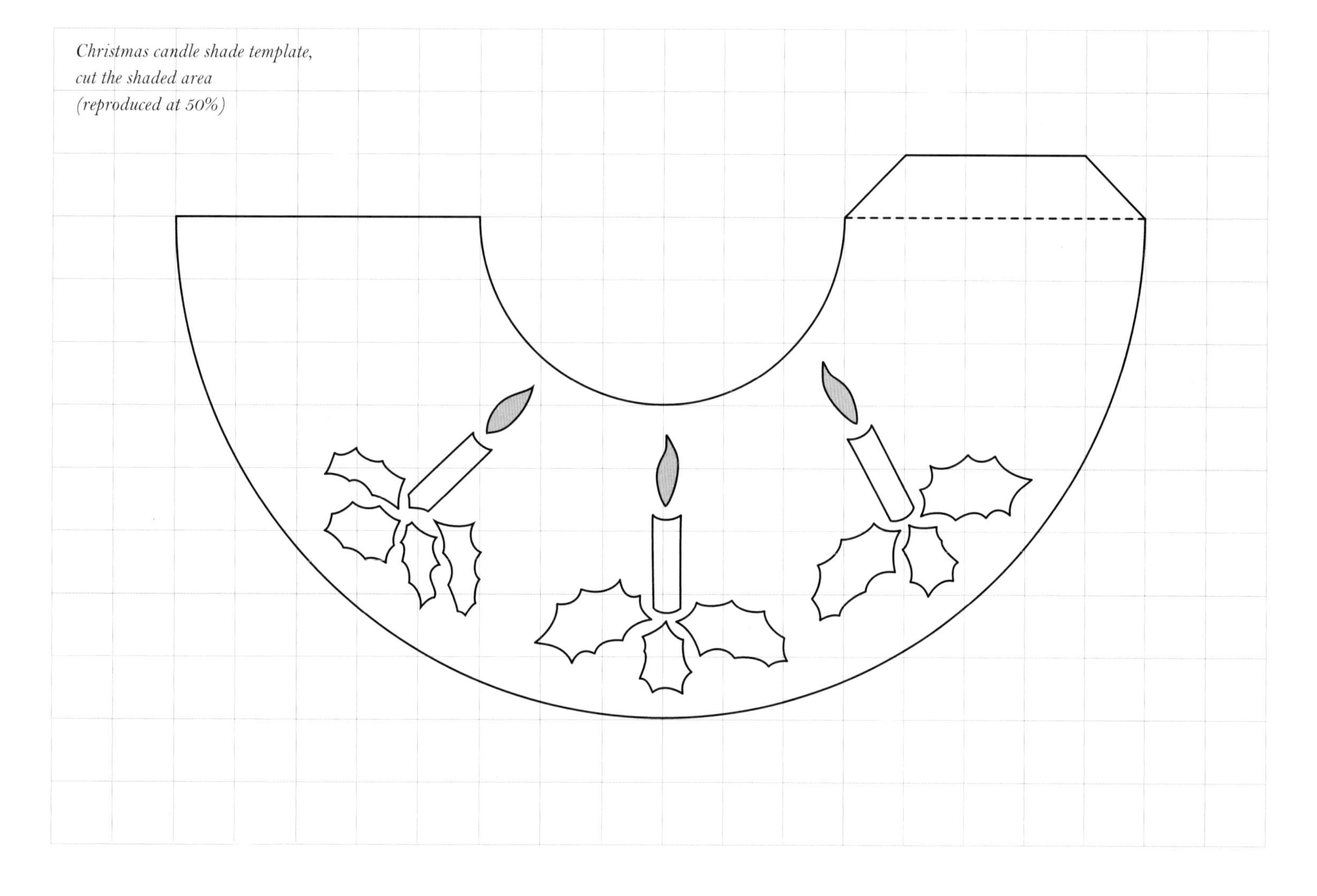

Christmas candle shade template, cut the shaded area (reproduced at 50%)

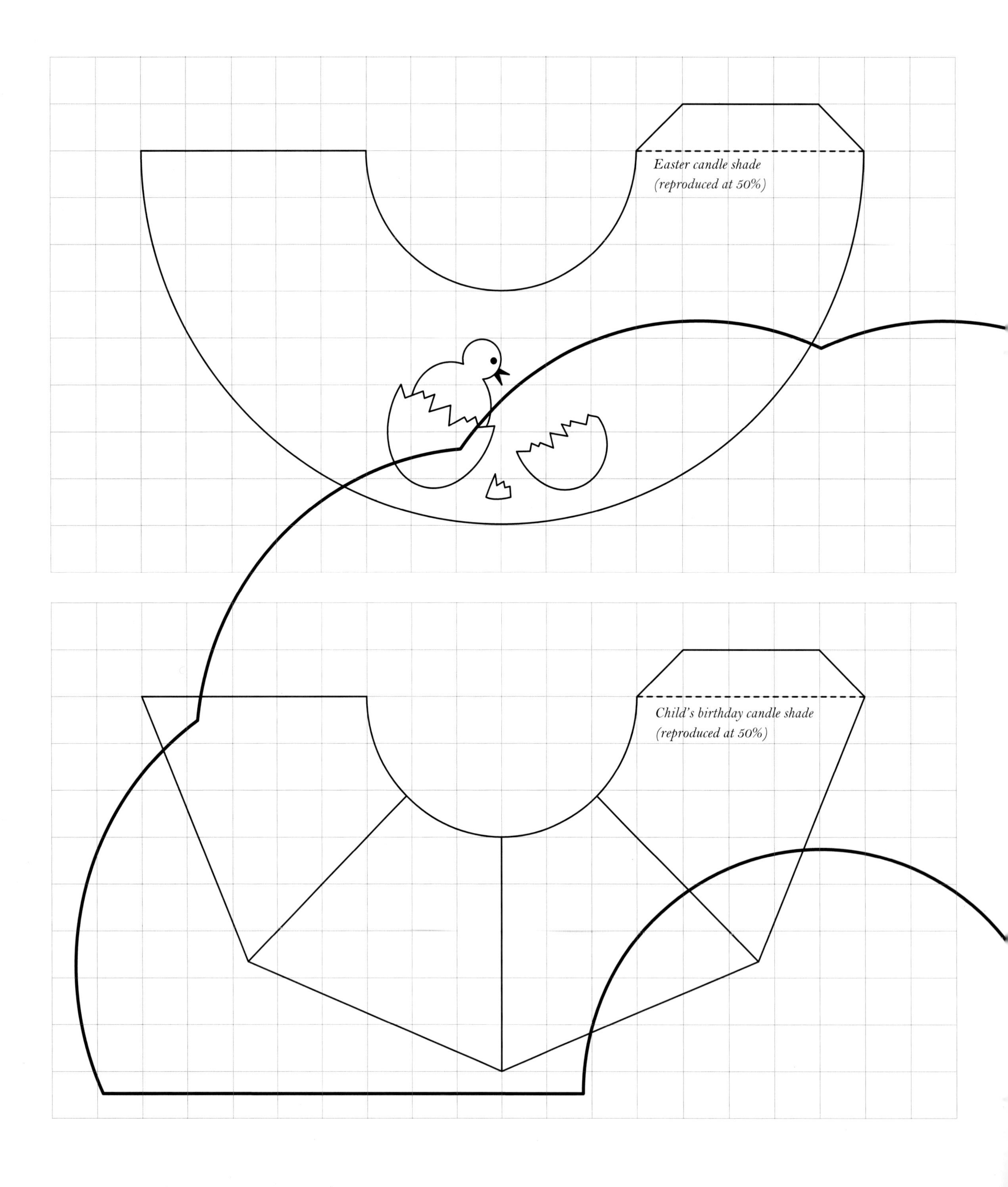
Easter candle shade
(reproduced at 50%)
Child's birthday candle shade
(reproduced at 50%)

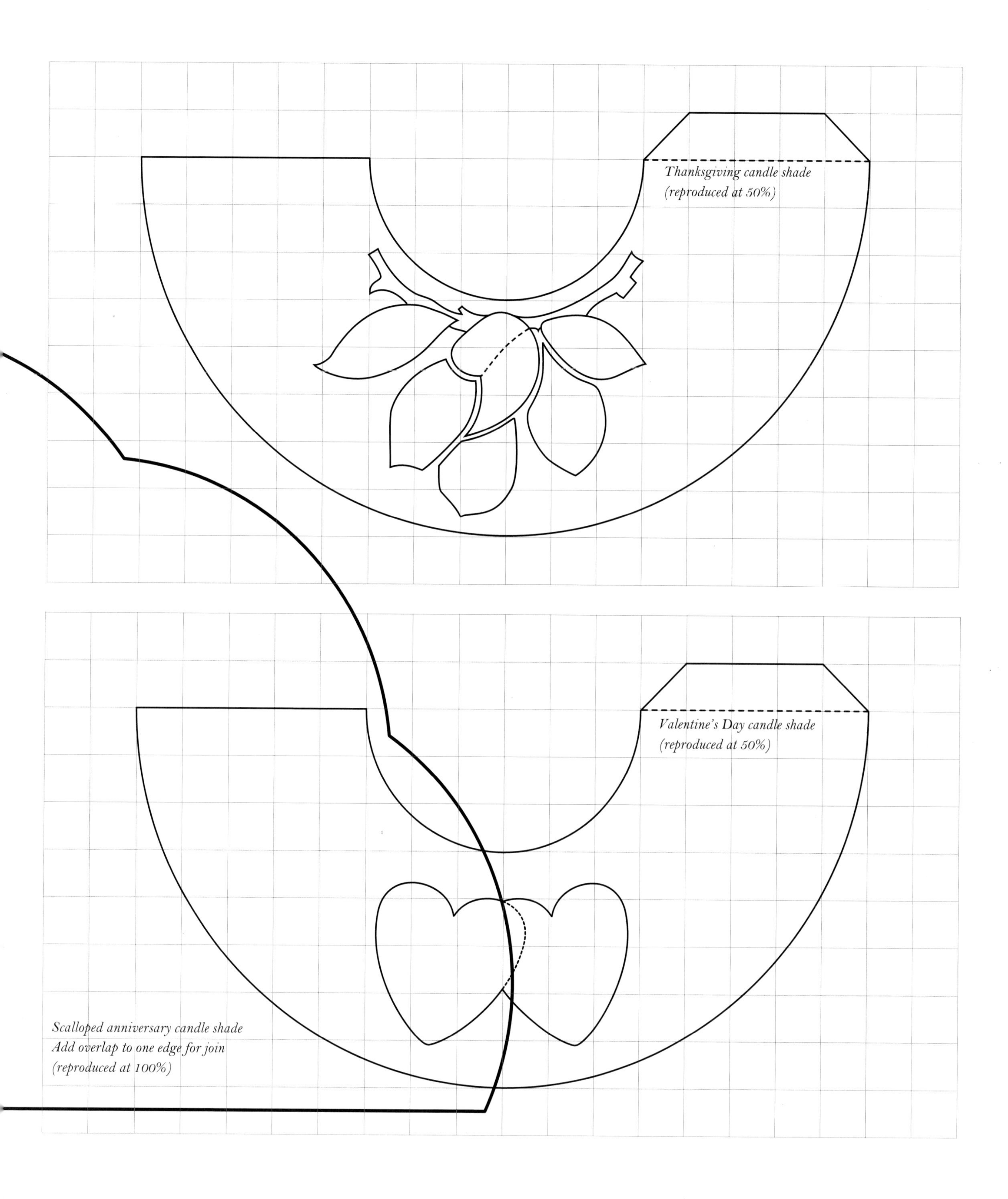
Thanksgiving candle shade
(reproduced at 50%)
Valentine's Day candle shade
(reproduced at 50%)
Scalloped anniversary candle shade
Add overlap to one edge for join
(reproduced at 100%)

Tarty Party

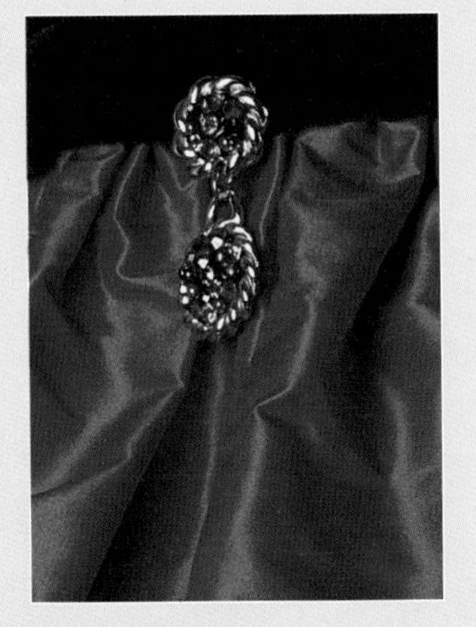

Parties are fun - so decoration can be as frivolous, over the top and "tarty" as you wish, keeping a sense of humour to the fore.

Here is a chance to play fairy godmother and let your lighting go to the ball. Slip-over shades in richly coloured fabrics are gathered and pleated to make "skirts" glamorised with beads, ribbons, bows, flowers, necklaces or earrings. Dense, dark fabrics create intimate pools of light; silks and taffetas gleaming in various corners of the room will give your party instant pzazz.

Choose colours, fabrics and trimmings to complement the occasion, balancing the food, the season and the house decorations. Deep reds, greens and terracotta in plush velvets and heavy shot silks will help to create a rich, warm atmosphere for Christmas or winter parties. Pale blue, pink, apricot or lemon, adorned with ribbons and fresh flowers make mouthwatering shades redolent of summer fruits and skies for wedding receptions and summer birthdays.

A visit to specialist ribbon and bead shops will inspire you, and remnants of glitzy fabrics are inexpensive. Or rummage through your fabric box - the pleated and shot silks and velvets used here were all remnants from my own skirts and cushions. These shades are one night stands - they don't have to last, they just have to provide a touch of theatre - none of those shown has been made using a machine, all took less than 30 minutes to complete.

VOL. I
VOL. I
BRUT

The basic technique for these shades involves joining a strip of fabric at the short ends to form a tube which is gathered to fit over the permanent lampshade. The two purple shades have been hemmed, one with shell stitches and the other using ribbon to cover the raw edges.The green and apricot shades were both made using two tubes joined together at the top. The top layers scrunch up to reveal the under skirts fixed in place with a paper, fabric or silk rose.

As long as you use the same coloured thread, back seams may be tacked together and gathering threads just pulled up and secured tightly, enough to last the evening. Fabric folded in half saves the need for a hem and bows and ribbons may be just pinned in place - pure theatre.

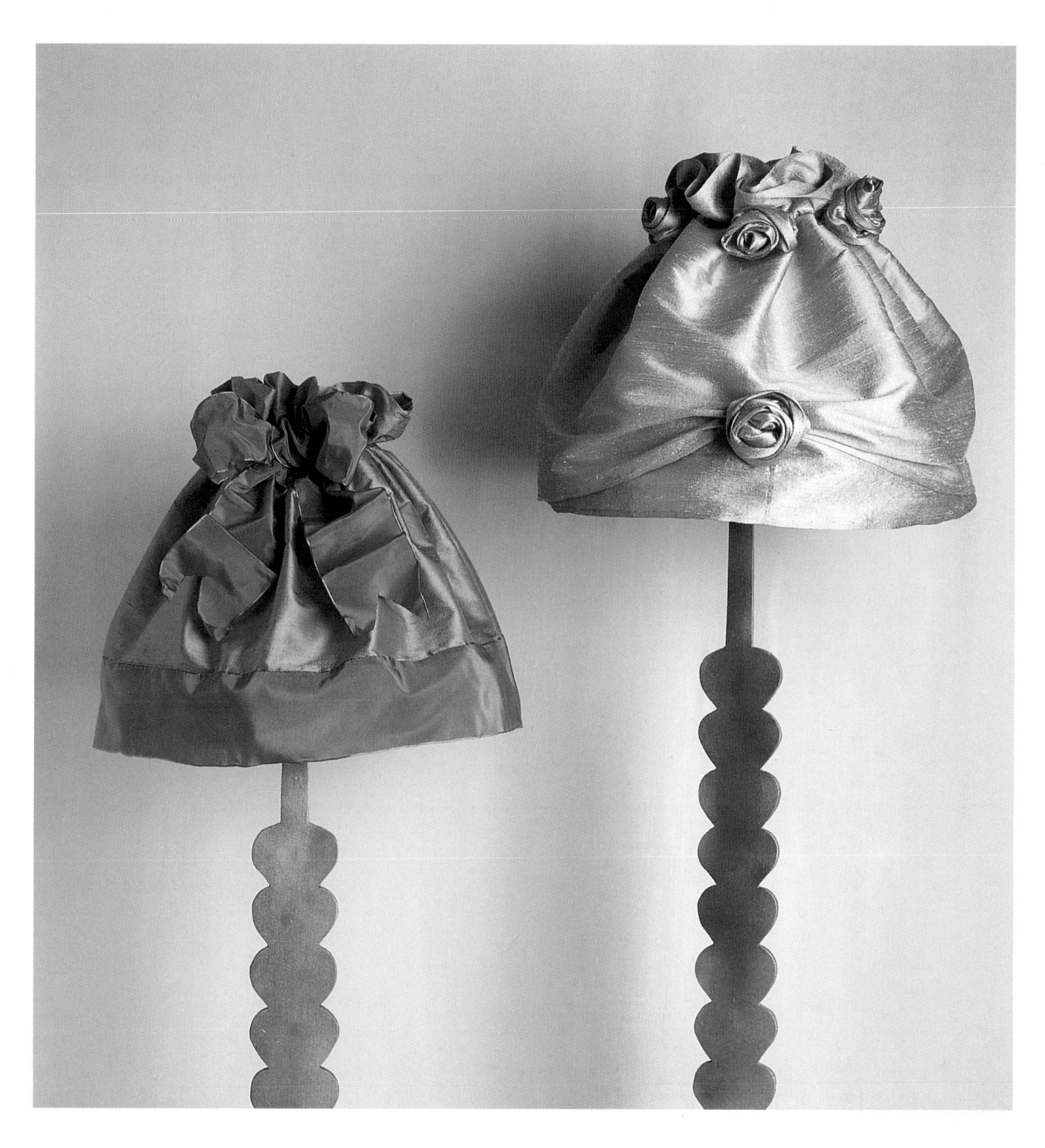

These shades were made with just a little fullness but the choice is yours, by design and how much fabric you have available, especially if you are using remnants. If you are giving a theme party or are making a quick cover for a birthday party or other celebration, you can really let your imagination run riot for your shade decoration. Search out small items from shops specialising in children's toys and jokes, from novelty and gift shops, cake decorating suppliers and stationers. These covers can be slipped over most shapes of shade.

Use taffetas, heavyweight silks and velvets in rich or vibrant colours. The beauty of good quality taffeta is the way you can scrunch it into interesting shapes which emphasise the wonderful depths of colour reflected in the folds as soft lamp light shines through.

YOU WILL NEED

- *card or fabric under shade*
- *top fabric, see below*
- *optional second fabric, see below*
- *decoration, such as beads, twisted rope, earrings, fabric or real flowers*

MEASURE

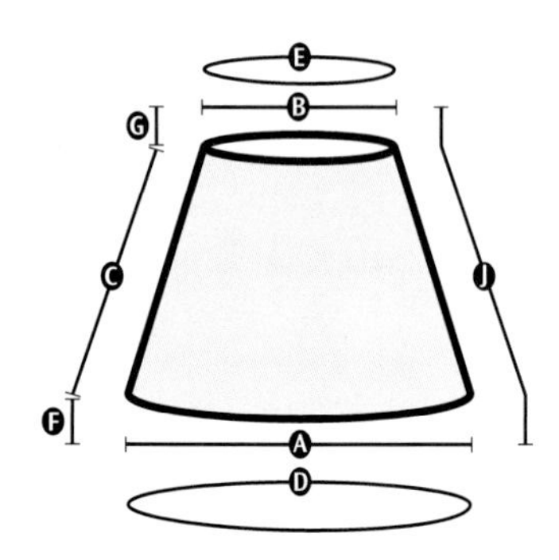

C = slope
D = base circumference
F = overhang
G = heading allowance

To find the fabric width, multiply the base circumference measurement by between one and a quarter and two times, depending on the fullness required.

For the depth, allow enough fabric for the frill at the top to fold over and add a seam allowance, so that the raw edge is included with the gathering threads (G x 2 + 2 cm/¾ in), e.g. a standing frill of 6 cm (2½ in) will need 14 cm (5¾ in) of fabric.To find the fabric depth, add together frill depth + C + F plus 2 cm (¾ in) hem allowance. If you prefer to fold the fabric in half using the foldline for the hem, double this measurement.

Basic party shade

A quick and easy shade for a one-off occasion, using one or two fabrics.

To make up

1 Cut one or both top fabrics, then join each strip of fabric along the short sides and press the seam open.

2 Hemstitch the lower edge or fold in half lengthwise leaving the fold to form the hemline. Fold the top over to give your chosen frill depth. Run two gathering threads round, the first approximately 0.5 cm (¼ in) from the raw edge and the other 2 cm (¾ in) from it and parallel to it. Pull up to fit the top of the under shade and secure. If you have time, make a fabric band (see page 125) and slip stitch over the gathering stitches.

Note: If you have chosen to use two layers of fabric, make each up independently and join together with the gathering threads.

3 Gather the lower edge into scallops and stitch in place at the back. Alternatively, if using two layers, draw up the top one and fasten in place with a decorative rose as described on the next page. Decorate the top with flowers, if liked.

Decorative bows

Use ribbons in silk organdie or taffeta, especially those with wired edges, which will bend into lovely folds and stay in shape. Cut scraps of fabric - silks, chintzes, velvets or tartans - and pink the edges or leave raw for just one occasion.

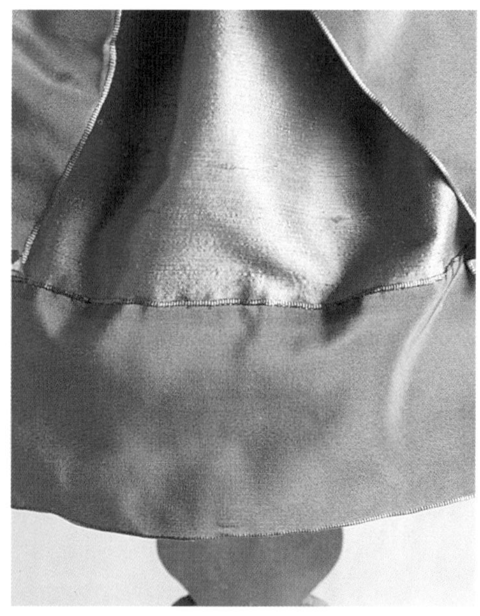

Decorative roses

Of course there is nothing to compare with the colour and perfume of real roses. If you are able to pick them from the garden, wrap damp cotton wool around the stems and cover with florist's ribbon or strips of silk, then pin in place for the evening.

Decorative roses are fairly expensive to buy but are easy to make from scraps of silks and ribbons. Cut pieces from 50 - 100 cm (18 - 36 in) long and tapering from 7 - 14 cm (3 - 6 in) in width. Fold in half lengthwise, neaten the raw edges and run a gathering thread close to and through both raw edges. Pull up to approximately half the length, then form into a roll, starting from the narrowest edge which will be the middle of the rose. Stitch securely at the base at each turn. Cover the raw edges at the back with a small hemmed square of fabric and finger the rose into a pretty shape. Pin or stitch to the shade.

Experiment with different-sized fabric strips to make either tight rosebuds or full blown roses.

Ribbon edges

Ribbons with very fine wire woven into one or both selvedges are also perfect for stitching along the hemline to hold full skirts in shape.

Evening Dress

These stunning slipcover shades put the accent on fabric, displaying the marvellous properties of silks and damasks.

That truly magnificent piece of damask or the odds and ends of luxurious shot silk that you have been saving for something special can now step into the limelight in creations reminiscent of renaissance Italy - or at least the wardrobe room of La Scala.

If the last chapter came out of the dressing-up box, this one has more in common with haute couture. Cut and detail matter here: taffeta is inset with damask, hems are scalloped, gold beads glint, silk swirls like an evening cloak on an opera goer. These shades are sensuous and sophisticated, the de Medicis of the world of lighting - they are not out on the town, they own the town.

The desired effect is opulent rather than flashy, these are permanent shades meant to balance other fine furnishings or temporary covers for seasonal and occasional change. Carefully chosen fabrics will ensure that you produce something that is unusual and interesting, but also comfortable to live with rather than dramatic and therefore tiring to the eye.

Choose subtle but warm colours in fabrics with a texture and sheen to them that catches the eye but does not dazzle it. Test different combinations before you start work and don't forget to look at them in the evening, when they will come into their own.

Damask, shot silk and brocade or combinations of these materials are eminently suitable. Gold drops, tiny piping and narrow ribbons add subtle decorative touches.

YOU WILL NEED

- *card or fabric under shade or stretched under shade*
- *dressmaker's pattern paper*
- *pair of compasses*
- *calico for toile*
- *fabric A for the flat sections and piping, see chart*
- *fabric B for the gores, see chart*
- *fabric A, B or organdie for lining, see chart*
- *00 piping cord*
- *fabric A or B for piping, see chart*
- *matching threads*
- *tape or ribbon for top binding, see chart*
- *lid (optional)*

Gored slipcover shade

I always appreciate the subtle contrast gained from using two toning fabrics and enjoy the vibrancy when two contrasting fabrics are worked together. You could, however, make the whole shade from one fabric, which would emphasise the shaping as the light reflects from the different surfaces.

To make up

1 Make a circle on the pattern paper using the slope of the shade as the radius. Divide and cut into eight equal segments for the gores.

2 Make a template of the under shade (see page 125) and divide into eight for the flat sections. Place one of each onto calico and draw around, adding 1.5 cm (5/8 in) seam allowance to all sides.

3 Make up a calico toile using eight flat panels and eight gores and tack them together along the seam allowances. Test to fit, and make any necessary adjustments. You might need to tidy up the top circle.

4 Using the toile as a pattern, cut out the gores in one fabric and the flat sections in the chosen contrast. Stitch together as the toile. Trim seams back to 1 cm (5/8 in) and press to the right. Make

up the lining in the same way, also pressing seams to the right. Make up the piping (see page 124) and pin to the right side of the skirt, along the hemline. Stitch in place. Pin the lining to the top fabric, right sides together, matching up all the seams. Stitch round the hemline from the wrong side (so that you can follow the piping stitching line), taking 1 cm (3/8 in) seam allowance. Press, turn right side out, press again and pin the tops together.

5 Self-bind the top to enclose all raw edges neatly (see page 125). Alternatively, enclose between two pieces of ribbon (see page 100). Place on the shade and turn up the triangular sections at the bottom of the slipcover.

Variation

This shade can easily be made as a permanent cover rather than a slipcover if you combine this method with a stretched cover. It is also suitable for a frame with a built-in lid - or, to make your own lid, just twist thin wires across the top of the frame to make a light, but strong support.

You will need to allow enough extra fabric of either A or B as follows: for the lid, top circumference times radius plus 3 cm (1 1/4 in); for the self binding, the length of the top circumference plus seam allowance and 3 cm (1 1/4 in) wide; for the stretched cover and for the lining (see page 12). For a 25 - 35.5 cm (10 - 14 in) shade allow 2 m (2 1/4 yds), for 40 - 45.5 cm (16 - 18 in) allow 2.5 m (3 yds) and for 51 - 56 cm (20 - 22 in) allow 3 m (3 1/2 yds).

Cut and make a tight lining (see page 122) and stretched top cover (page 12) using fabric A or B as chosen. Pin and stitch to the frame. Make up the gored shade as on page 78 (steps 1 to 4). Pin the wire lid to the top of the shade and stitch securely with lampshade stitches. Pin the lid fabric all round the circumference and stitch. Pleat to the centre and stitch the pleats to the wire. Trim excess fabric. Make a fabric-covered button and stitch in place to hide all raw edges.

Press the self-binding strip into three, open out and stitch round the top of the gored shade, along the bottom fold line of the binding. Join the short ends. Fold the other raw edge inside and stitch along the top fold with tiny stitches.

GORED SLIP COVERS *(inches)*

Empire shades are the most suitable for this style of cover.

Frame size A x B x C	*number of sections*	*Fabric A flat sections*	*Fabric B Gores*	*top binding*	*base binding/piping*
8 x 4 x 6	8	45 x 14	54 x 14	14	66
10 x 5 x 7	8	45 x 14	54 x 14	17	77
12 x 6 x 8	10	45 x 14	54 x 14	20	92
14 x 7 x 9	10	54 x 14	80 x 14	23	104
16 x 8 x 10	10	64 x 16	80 x 16	27	117
18 x 10 x 12	12	64 x 16	80 x 16	33	136
20 x 11 x 13	12	90 x 20	98 x 20	36	148
22 x 12 x 14	12	90 x 20	98 x 20	39	160
24 x 14 x 16	12	90 x 20	98 x 20	45	180

GORED SLIP COVERS *(centimetres)*

Frame size A x B x C	*number of sections*	*Fabric A flat sections*	*Fabric B Gores*	*top binding*	*base binding/piping*
20 x 10 x 15	8	114 x 35.5	137 x 35.5	35.5	168
25 x 12.5 x 18	8	114 x 35.5	137 x 35.5	43	196
30 x 15 x 20	10	114 x 35.5	137 x 35.5	51	234
35.5 x 18 x 23	10	137 x 35.5	203 x 35.5	58.5	264
40 x 20 x 25	10	163 x 40	203 x 40	69	297
45.5 x 25 x 30	12	163 x 40	203 x 40	84	345
51 x 28 x 33	12	229 x 51	249 x 51	92	376
56 x 30 x 35.5	12	229 x 51	249 x 51	99	407
61 x 35.5 x 40	12	229 x 51	249 x 51	115	457

Lining
For ease, add fabrics A and B together or for economy, place pieces onto a table and plan a tighter cut as lining pieces can be dovetailed.

Base binding
Cut on the cross and 6 cm (2 1/2 in) wide for a 1.5 cm (5/8 in) binding.

Top binding
Use bought tape or fabric folded over to 2 cm (3/4 in) finished width, so cut length as chart and 8 cm (3 in) wide.

A perfectly easy slipcover shade to make from panels stitched together and tied round the top of a card or fabric under shade (*left*). Suitable for almost any empire or Pembroke shades, the generous skirt can be fitted to disguise or emphasise the shape beneath.

This shade is a variation of the one described in detail on page 94. It is lined and piped at top and bottom. Tiny 00 piping makes a very neat finish for a lined shade. Make up the lining and top fabric with flat seams, just leaving one of the lining seams mostly open. Stitch the piping to the top cover round the top and bottom edges, snipping into the shaping so that the piping lies flat. Place the top fabric and lining, right sides together and stitch all round following the piping stitching line and stitch just inside for a really tight finish. Turn right side out through the lining seam. Press, then slipstitch the opening together.

1

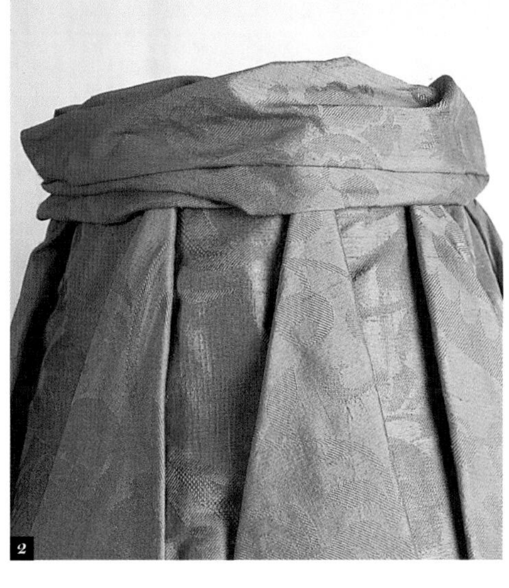

2

This shade (*far left*) is made in exactly the same way as described on page 78. You will need to make and fit a tight lining to the frame (page 122). Fit the gored shade to the top of the frame and stitch all round with lampshade stitches. Stitch each flat section to the bottom of the frame and finger press each gored section flat so that they all meet. Stitch fabric-covered or other buttons over each meeting, securing both folds to the frame beneath (1). Twist a length of spare fabric round the top and hand stitch in place (2).

Two layers in toning silks allow varying degrees of light to shine through (*right*). To make a circular underskirt, measure from the centre of the top of the frame to the required length past the bottom of the shade and cut a fabric circle using this measurement for the radius. Finish the top with self-binding or ribbon and stitch a shell hem (see page 124).

To make the top skirt, cut a template to the size of the shade (see page 125), divide into 8 sections and shape the lower edge of each into a point. Cut away the top 5 cm (2 in) and pin together along the side seams. Fit over the circular skirt and re-pin each seam to taper more until the top fits neatly. Stitch seams, line, turn out and finish with a self-binding (page 125).

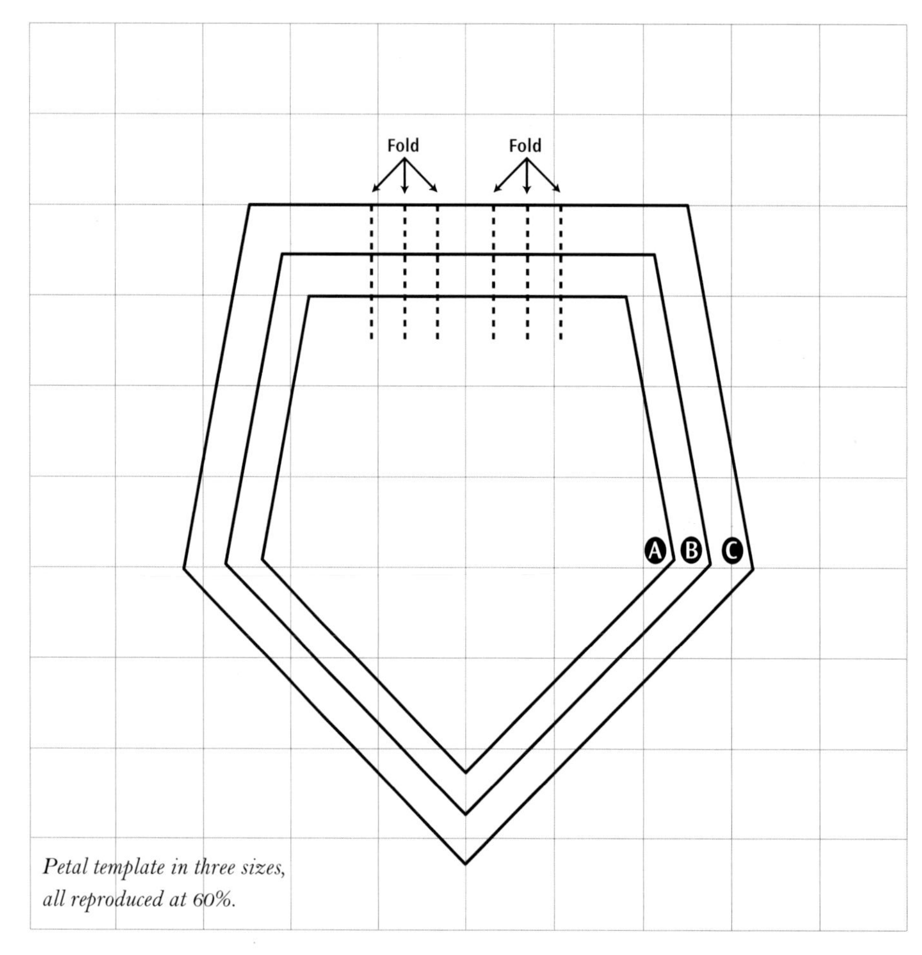

Petal template in three sizes, all reproduced at 60%.

Petal-trimmed slipcover

A good cover to slip over any light-coloured silk or painted card shade, the main skirt is made from a doubled-over tube, just one and a quarter times the circumference of the base of the under shade. Petals in two colours were stitched to the top of the tube and the whole pleated into a self-binding to fit comfortably over the top of the under shade. This cover is shown over a pleated empire frame but could be adapted for a coolie, stretched, dome and almost any round frame.

Cut fabric to twice the required finished depth and one and a quarter time fullness. Pin the excess fullness round the top into twelve pleats spaced at equal distances. To make the petals, use the template on page 82 which best suits your frame, add seam allowances all round, then cut out 12 pieces for the fronts and 12 for the backs. Either join these to form a long strip or make up individually. Stitch the backs carefully to the fronts, keeping the points sharp. Neaten the seams and turn right sides out.

Press into neat shapes and pin to the top of the skirt. Fold each to fit, so that the petal folds line up with the skirt folds. Stitch together and finish with a self binding. Tweak the fabric pieces into petal-like forms, using spray starch to stiffen for a more permanent effect or to help a floppy fabric.

These petal templates will fit:
A) a frame with top diameter up to 15 cm (6 in) and tube circumference approximately 100 cm (40 in),
B) a frame with top diameter up to 20 cm (8 in) and tube circumference approximately 135 cm (54 in),
C) a frame with top diameter up to 28 cm (11 in) and tube circumference approximately 180 cm (70 in).

If your frame falls outside these categories, adjust the template up or down or cut more or fewer petals. Experiment with calico or paper.

Shot silks make the most pleasing lampshade covers. During the daytime, light reflects from the top and from deep within the folds to show the richness of colours both in shadow and in full light. Once the lamp is switched on, the light shines through from behind, bringing the colours to life in a completely new way.

The lampshade in the photograph on page 30 has been taken in exactly the same setting to show how these slipcovers work. Creamy silk gives good reading light but might be too harsh for the evening, so unpin the tassels and pop a rich silk cover over to subdue the light for a cosy, late dinner.

This shade is made with a skirt only slightly fuller than the base circumference of the under shade, pleated at the top into self-binding, which is then tucked inside the frame. A contrast border has been added to the bottom, decorated with gold drops stitched at intervals to the top and bottom.

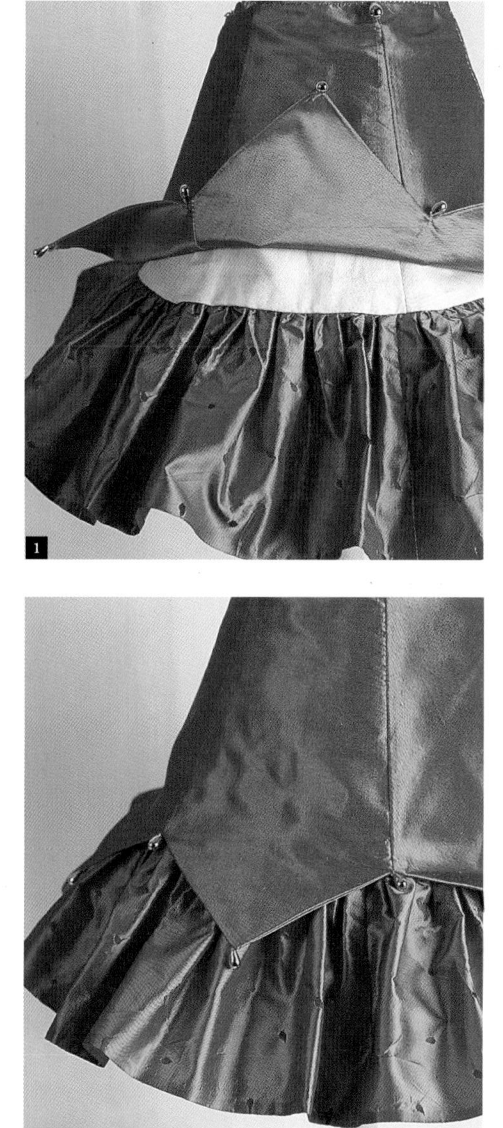

Flared skirt

A fun shade for a light-hearted touch to an evening occasion.

Make a template for the shade (see page 125) and cut into six sections. Cut one to make the pattern for the top skirt, make a point, keeping the centre the length of the template and tapering the sides to approximately 7.5 cm (3 in) up. Add seam allowances and cut twelve in silk. Join two sets of six, pin together, with right sides facing, and stitch round the lower edge, carefully keeping the points true. Trim the seams, turn right side out and press the points well. Pin together round the top. Cut 10 cm (4 in) off another section to make the lining template, cut out six and join together. Make a frill, approximately 15 cm (6 in) deep and three times the circumference of the bottom of the shade. Hem one long side and gather the other on to the lining (1).

Join the under skirt and top skirt together along the top edge, fit to the shade and finish with self-binding (see page 125). Stitch gold drops to each point (2) and to the seams at the top of the shade.

Whiter Than White

Standard lamps of this stature are supposed to be dressed with elegant stretched shades, elaborately decorated and finished with layers of heavy fringing and metres of braiding. In tune with the free spirit of the 90's, I chose to make a slipcover summer shade supported by a lined frame. Two layers of white fabric: one rough linen and one spotted organza, are gathered together and shaped with the help of lightly wired selvedges. They are tied in place with double bows made from polka dot voile.

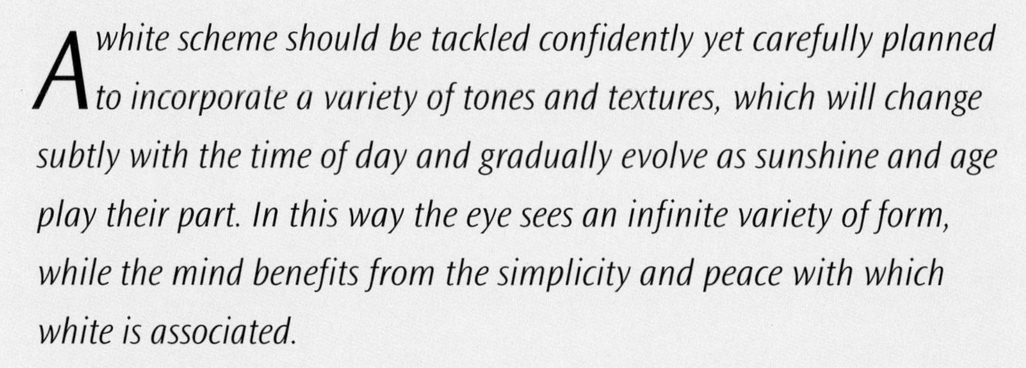

A white scheme should be tackled confidently yet carefully planned to incorporate a variety of tones and textures, which will change subtly with the time of day and gradually evolve as sunshine and age play their part. In this way the eye sees an infinite variety of form, while the mind benefits from the simplicity and peace with which white is associated.

White's popularity may have less to do with its therapeutic properties than with the omnipresence of white paints, fabrics and accessories - it is easy to find and always in fashion. Many people choose white because it seems safe (i.e. it won't "clash" with anything) and they forget that it has qualities of its own. It adapts to its surroundings, whether dazzling in tropical sunshine or providing nuances of grey and violet in the softer light of northern countries.

White shades, therefore, contribute more than just a good light to work by. They look striking against richly toned woods, ethereal over glass and homely over a ceramic base. Filmy organza shades look marvellous as a complete contrast to a very smart room or magical trimmed with roses in a chintz room. Whether inspiration is taken from pearls, fresh snow and crisp linen sheets, or from antique lace and yellowing manuscripts, white is never simply a soft option.

The discipline of using white can inspire really effective use of shape, texture and contrast. Silks, fine cottons and linens, organdie, muslin and organza adorned with ribbons, buttons, frills or crystal drops can be made into shades that are formal and crisp or friendly and feminine.

White lampshades can be created to suit almost any situation - crunchy linen trimmed with tiger skin ribbon might grace even the smartest dining table.

All of these fabrics have a life of their own: organdie keeps its shape beautifully; silk can be soft and floppy or scrunchy and resilient; linen will wash and wash but is inclined to crease.

YOU WILL NEED

- *card or fabric under shade*
- *cotton organdie for top skirt and bow, see below*
- *lawn or fine linen for under skirt, see below*
- *50 cm (18 in) linen, heavy cotton or velvet for the collar*
- *matching thread*
- *crystal drops*

MEASURE

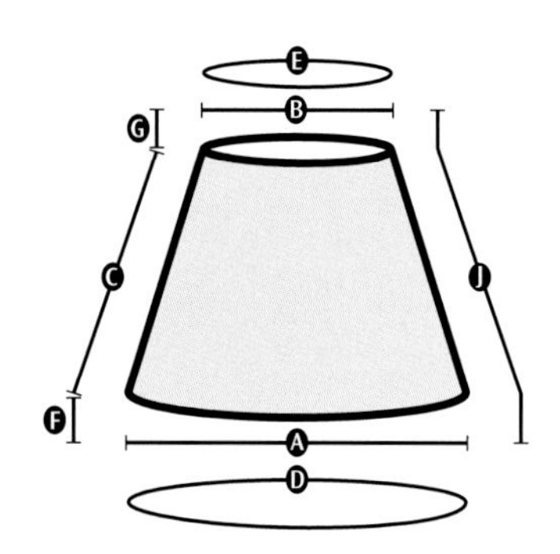

C = slope
D = base circumference

Measure two and a half to three times the base circumference for the width, depending on how full you want the slipcover to be. For the depth, measure the slope and add 10.5 cm (4⅛ in).

The template on page 92 will fit a coolie shade 30 x 10 x 18 cm (12 x 4 x 7 in). To make a collar for any shade, follow the instructions on page 125 for making a template and divide into sections as required. Adjust this template, making the points shorter, longer, narrower or wider to fit your shade.

Double-skirted slipcover shade with pointed collar

Organza, linen and crystal drops on an elegant glass base bring the perfect feminine touch to a smart dining room. This light, airy slipcover could be made up in fine cotton velvet for a stylish winter alternative.

To make up

1 To make the skirt, cut two layers of fabric, one from cotton organdie, the other from linen or lawn. Join the short sides of each with tiny French seams and press. Make small rolled hems, stitching with the smallest hand or machine stitches and press. Pin the two tubes together placing the organza skirt, so that it is just 3 mm (⅛ in) longer than the lining (1).

2 Pin securely all along the top and fold under the heading allowance of 3.5 cm (1⅜ in). Run a gathering thread through both layers 2 cm (¾ in) from the top and another 1.5 cm (⅝ in) below. Pull up to fit the top of the under shade and finish with a fabric-covered band (see page 125).

3 To make the collar, cut two pieces of linen, cotton or velvet using the template on page 92 and place right sides together. Pin all round. Stitch round the top and along the bottom edge 1 cm (⅜ in) in from the raw edge. Stop the needle at each point and turn the fabric in the machine before continuing along the next section to keep the points sharp. Snip around the top curve and well into the points on the bottom edge (2).

4 Turn right side out and press. Use a pin or darning needle to make good points. Slip stitch the short edges together. Tack the small pleats in place. Pin the collar round the skirt and sit both on the shade. Adjust the tacked pleats if necessary. Remove the collar and stitch the pleats, then stitch a crystal drop to each of the points (3). Fit the collar back over the two skirts on the under shade.

5 Tie a bow with an offcut of fabric to judge how much is needed, then use this width and length to make one in the organdie.

1

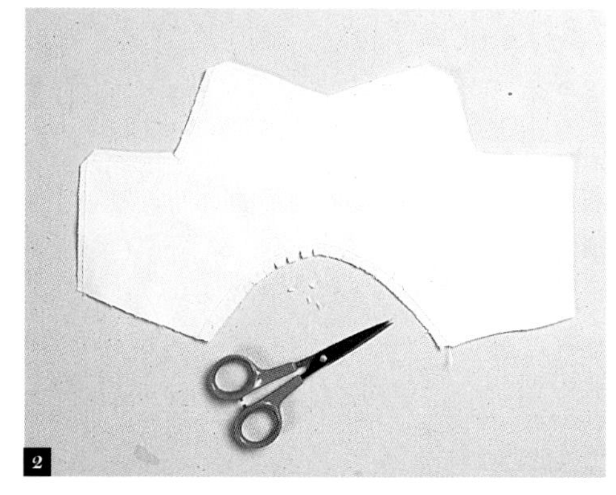

2

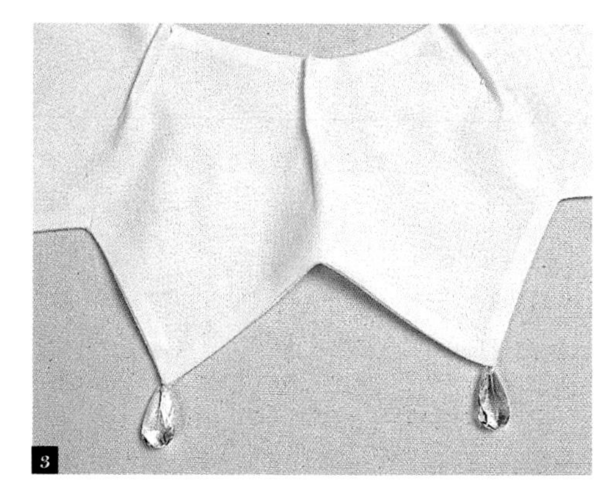

3

Pink roses

I made this shade for a class of students to prove it really is possible to make a shade in approximately twenty minutes. I cut one length of fabric one and a half times the base circumference and 11 cm (4¼ in) longer than the depth of the under shade. Hand stitching the short sides together with a French seam (see page 124) and rolling and slip stitching the hem as I went, saved pressing, marking and pinning time - a process which should not be missed unless you are used to handling fabrics. I folded back 6 cm (2½ in) at the top and ran a gathering thread along the length 1 cm (⅜ in) above the raw edge, pulled it up to fit the top of the under shade and secured it with a double stitch. I used a piece of frame binding tape to slip-stitch quickly round to hold the gathers in place inside and to cover the raw edge. Silk roses were made from handy offcuts (see page 73 for lovely, easy fabric roses).

I must admit that the inside would have benefited from a little more time, if I am to follow my own teaching, which demands that everything should look as good inside as it does outside!

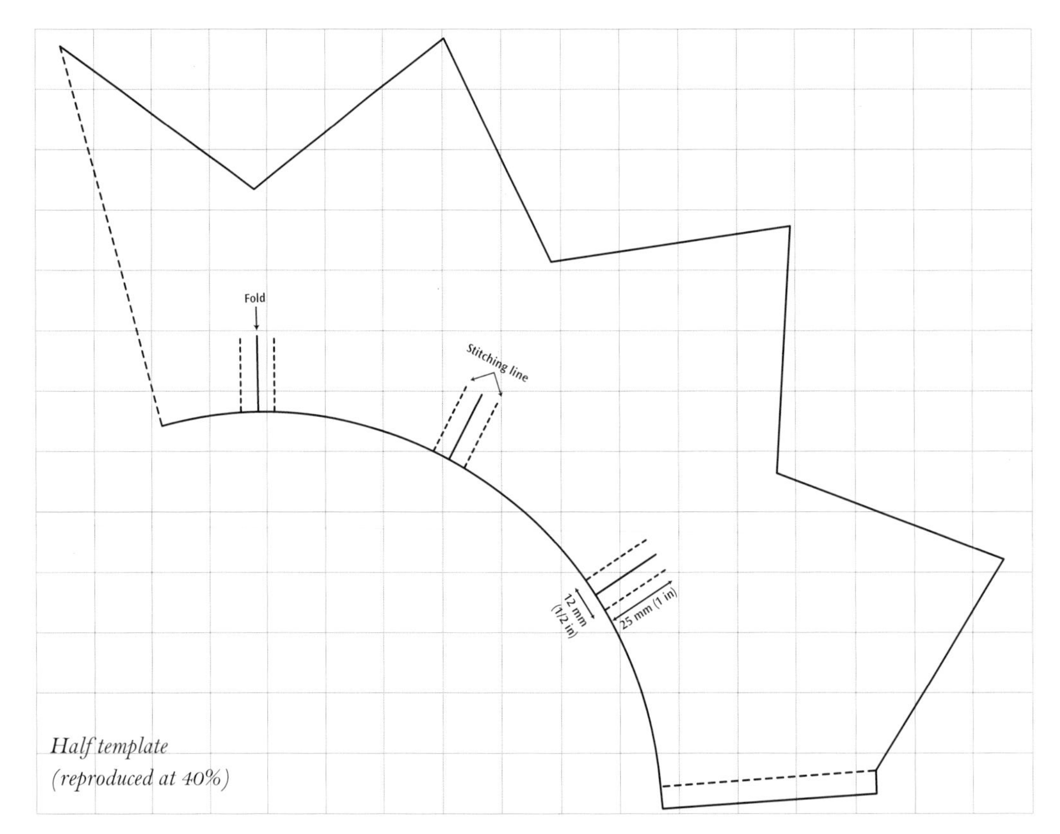

Half template (reproduced at 40%)

This shade (*left*) has just one skirt made from white teatowel linen. Zebra-skin ribbon is used to make the fabric-covered band at the top; to trim the bottom of the skirt and to form the long-tailed bow.

Fine white linen trimmed with cascades of fluffy cotton bobbles (bought in a length) and tied up with a black ribbon makes a fun "still life" on a side table (*right*). This slipcover shade is made with a single skirt cut long enough to provide the flopped-over frill at the top.

Hand-painted buttons found at a local craft fair complement the simple gingham bow tie over layers of organdie and cotton (*left*).

YOU WILL NEED

- *card or fabric under shade*
- *dressmaker's pattern paper, for template*
- *calico for toile*
- *silk, cotton or linen for top cover, see chart*
- *contrast fabric to bind top and bottom, see chart*
- *ribbon or fabric tie*
- *lining fabric, e.g. silk, cotton or linen in same weight as top cover (optional), see chart*

Simple flared slipcover

Designed to fit over a gently sloping under shade, this slipcover is made from eight sections drawn up with a ribbon. If made with a contrast lining, it becomes reversible. A variation is shown on page 81.

To make up

1 Using dressmaker's pattern paper, make a template (see page 125) and divide into six or eight sections, according to the size of your under shade.

2 Lay one section on the calico and draw round, adding one and a half times the fullness across the width, 3 cm (1¼ in) at top and bottom and shaping as shown in the diagram opposite.

3 Cut out a total of six or eight pieces in calico to this shape, tack together and fit over your shade, using ribbon or a fabric scrap to gather it in at the top. If you like the length, shape and fullness, go ahead, if not, re-shape until you are satisfied with the fit.

4 Using the toile as a pattern, cut out the top fabric and lining, if used. Join the top fabric sections together with the smallest French seams possible. If lined, make 1 cm (⅜ in) flat seams, then press and pin the top fabric and lining fabrics, right sides together, and make up as one.

5 Bind the top and bottom edges with strips of fabric 4 cm (1½ in) wide cut on the cross (see page 124). Tie the slip-cover onto the under shade with a fabric tie or with ribbon. Spread the gathers evenly and stitch the ribbon or tie to the shade at each seam.

The instructions for making this gored shade (above) are given on page 78. The edge can be piped or bound, left plain or turned up in peaks. Dress the top with buttons or a folded collar.

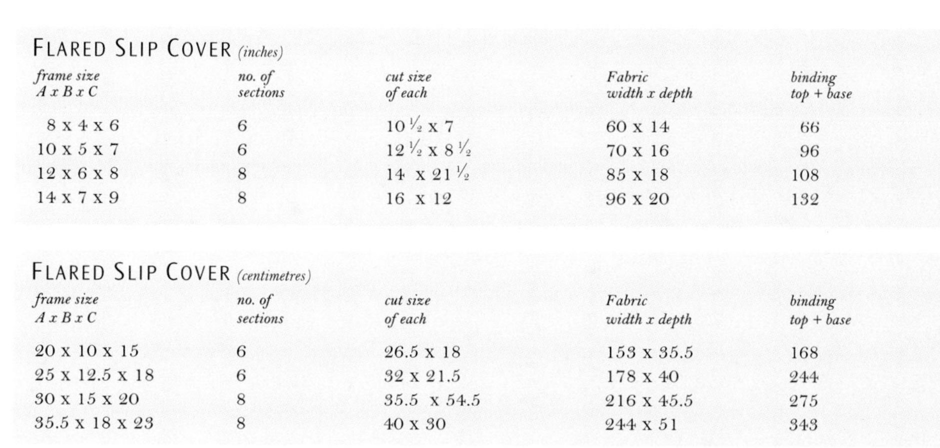

FLARED SLIP COVER *(inches)*

frame size A x B x C	*no. of sections*	*cut size of each*	*Fabric width x depth*	*binding top + base*
8 x 4 x 6	6	10½ x 7	60 x 14	66
10 x 5 x 7	6	12½ x 8½	70 x 16	96
12 x 6 x 8	8	14 x 21½	85 x 18	108
14 x 7 x 9	8	16 x 12	96 x 20	132

FLARED SLIP COVER *(centimetres)*

frame size A x B x C	*no. of sections*	*cut size of each*	*Fabric width x depth*	*binding top + base*
20 x 10 x 15	6	26.5 x 18	153 x 35.5	168
25 x 12.5 x 18	6	32 x 21.5	178 x 40	244
30 x 15 x 20	8	35.5 x 54.5	216 x 45.5	275
35.5 x 18 x 23	8	40 x 30	244 x 51	343

Summer Garden

All these shades are simply gathered tubes which slip over a plain card under shade.

A profusion of hollyhocks and roses, honeysuckle, daisies and violets has been drawn and redrawn, coloured and recoloured, printed and reprinted as our passion for the garden has brought the outside in.

Blowsy, faded chintzes have come to embody English decorating all over the world - reinterpreted as often in sophisticated city apartments as in country weekend retreats. The style, with its timeless fabrics, evokes a sense of security and comfort, recreating the romance of the past. "Pleasing decay" was the way John Fowler, perhaps the greatest English decorator, described the lived-in look of his ostensibly uncontrived interiors.

Chintz may rampage over the walls, bed, chairs and drapes of an entire bedroom or it may be pruned back to a single cushion or lamp-shade punctuating an all-white sitting room. Summer chintzes layered with simple checks and lace trims resembling old-fashioned petticoats can not only dress windows and cushions but also be made into multi-skirted lampshades.

Think of summer tea among the herbaceous borders, cosy week-ends in picture postcard cottages, a scrubbed pine dresser laden with blue and white china, shelves trimmed with lace and the colours of rustic spongeware. These are the images to keep in mind when choosing fabrics to create colourful slipcovered shades to drop neatly over card under shades.

These simply made slipcovers drop onto card or pleated shades, perhaps to disguise a worn-out shade or to provide summer colours for a welcome seasonal change. Frills and bows, tiny piped edges, smart shirt-striped linings and simple checks complement and contrast with fresh and faded chintzes; ribbons and buttons, braid and lace trims, reminiscent of summer party frocks, complete the effect.

Match lightweight cottons with contrasting patterns, such as checks and stripes or florals and stripes. Floral chintzes with a pale background are also very good teamed with a small amount of plain glazed cotton picking out one of the colours for any piping used to add subtle detail to edges.

Triple skirted and gathered slipcover

The three layers shown here are organza for the underskirt, striped cotton for the middle and floral for the top.

To make up

1 Cut out the three fabrics. The organza underskirt has been made with three times fullness and is cut double to hang 12 cm (5 in) below the under shade. The other two skirts have one and a half times fullness and are cut just 2 cm (¾ in) longer than the under shade. The top skirt also has an 8 cm (3¼ in) allowance.for the frill.

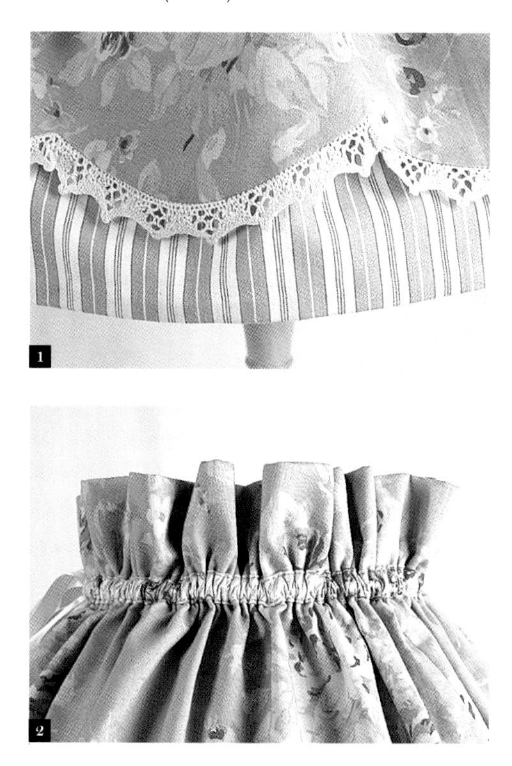

2 To make up the organza underskirt, join the short sides with a tiny French seam, then press in half lengthwise with the seam inside. Run a gathering thread 1.5 cm (⅝ in) down from the top edge and pull up to fit the top of the under shade. To bind the top, cut two pieces of ribbon 2 cm (¾ in) longer than the top circumference. Pin one to the front of the skirt with the bottom edge aligning with the line of gathering. Hem stitch in position along the bottom edge to hold the gathers in place. Fold over the ends of the ribbon to neaten the join. Stitch the other piece of ribbon to the inside in the same way, then stitch the two together along the top to fully enclose the raw edges. Place this skirt over the under shade.

3 To make the top skirt, place the cut length onto the worktable and press. Using a pencil, draw round a saucer, small bowl or other household object to make a scalloped hem. Trim the width, so that you have full scallops. Stitch the lace just above the drawn line (so that the pencil line is securely within the seam allowance and the lace is lying away from the seam

allowance). Trim the fabric to within 1 cm (⅜ in) of the stitching line.

4 Cut a facing as deep as the scallops plus seam allowances. Neaten one edge. Place on the worktable with the scalloped fabric on top, right sides together. Pin and stitch together round the scallops, following the stitching line. Trim excess fabric to within 1 cm (⅜ in) of the stitching line. Join the short sides and press the seams flat. Snip into the angles round the scallops, then turn to the inside and press.

5 To make the middle skirt, press under 1 cm (⅜ in) along the bottom edge, then another 1 cm (⅜ in) to make a hem. Hem stitch picking up single threads only. Pin to the top skirt, keeping the scallops just above the hemline (1).

6 Pin together at the top. Fold over 8 cm (3¼ in) at the top of the top skirt to make a frilled heading and to enclose the raw edge from the top of the middle skirt. Fold the raw edge under and pin.

7 To make a channel for the tie, cut a strip of fabric to the circumference of the skirt and 2.5 cm (1 in) deep. Press the raw edges to the middle to make it 1.25 cm (½ in) wide and neaten the ends, then stitch onto the front of the shade along both edges, positioning the bottom edge against the fold line of the heading. Leave a 5 mm (¼ in) gap instead of joining. Make up a fabric rouleau or use ribbon and thread through the channel. Pull up to fit the top of the shade (2), tie into a bow and slip over the organza skirt.

HEADING FRILL

depth *in*	*cm*	*add to skirt length* *in*	*cm*
1	2.5	2½	6
1½	3.5	3	8
1¾	4.0	4	10
2	4.5	5	12
2¼	5.5	6	14

BASE FRILL

Cut twice the depth of the finished frill plus 3 cm (1¼ in) and three times width of slipcover

GATHERED SHADES *(inches)*

frame size *A x B x C*	*fabric depth*	*fabric width fullness*	*fullness*	*fullness*	*fullness*	*top binding*
		1.25	**1.5**	**1.75**	**2.00**	
6 x 3 x 5	8	24	29	34	38	12
8 x 4 x 6	9	31	38	44	50	13
10 x 5 x 7	10	40	48	56	64	16
12 x 6 x 8	11	47	57	66	76	19
14 x 7 x 9	12	55	66	77	88	22
16 x 8 x 10	13	64	77	90	103	26
18 x 10 x 12	15	71	85	100	114	32
20 x 11 x 13	16	79	94	110	126	35
22 x 12 x 14	17	87	105	123	140	38

GATHERED SHADES *(centimetres)*

frame size *A x B x C*	*fabric depth*	*fabric width fullness*	*fullness*	*fullness*	*fullness*	*top binding*
		1.25	**1.5**	**1.75**	**2.00**	
15 x 7.5 x 12.5	20	61	74	86	97	30
20 x 10 x 15	23	79	97	112	127	33
25 x 12.5 x 18	25	102	122	142	163	40
30 x 15 x 20	28	120	145	168	193	48.5
35.5 x 18 x 23	30	140	168	196	224	56
40 x 20 x 25	33	163	196	229	262	66
45.5 x 25 x 30	38	180	216	254	290	81
51 x 28 x 33	40	201	239	280	320	89
56 x 30 x 35.5	43	221	267	313	356	96.5

Cut top binding 6 cm (2⅜ in) wide on the straight or cross

YOU WILL NEED

- *card or fabric under shade*
- *fabric for top skirt plus extra for facing, see chart*
- *fabric for middle skirt, see chart*
- *fabric for under skirt, see chart*
- *ribbon for top binding, see method*
- *1 m (1 yd) ribbon, 1.5 cm (⅝ in) wide or fabric rouleau (see page 125), for tie*
- *saucer or other round object*
- *narrow lace*

MEASURE

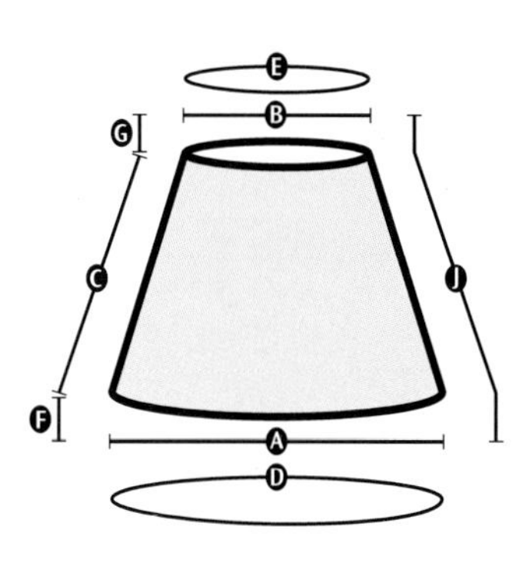

A = base diameter
B = top diameter
C = slope
D = base circumference
E = top circumference
F = hem allowance
G = heading allowance

Gathered fabric shades can be as full as you wish - but allow at least one and a quarter times the base circumference. Three times will give a very full cover and perhaps should be reserved for the finest lawns, silks and organza. The cover should fit neatly over the shade beneath and the bottom hem should hang between 2 and 6 cm (¾ and 2½ in) below the shade, depending on its size.

YOU WILL NEED

- *card or fabric under shade*
- *top fabric for skirt, binding and frill, as chart on page 101*
- *lining fabric, as chart on page 101*
- *00 piping*
- *piping fabric (see page 124)*
- *contrast marking thread*

MEASURE

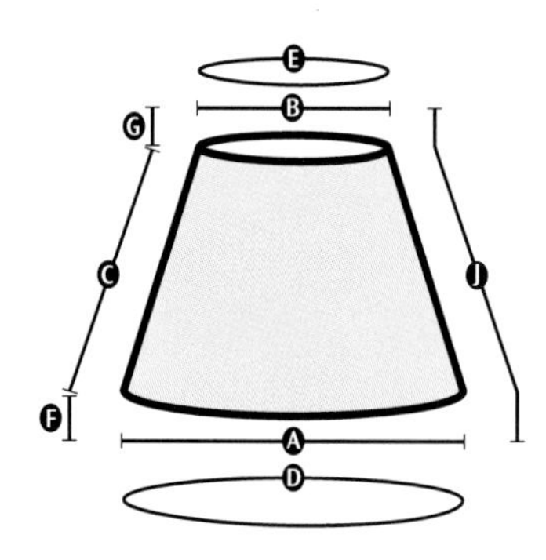

C = slope
D = base circumference
E = top circumference
F = hem allowance
G = heading allowance

Measure one and a quarter times the base circumference for the width of the skirt and lining. For the depth, measure the slope of the under shade and add 4 cm (1½ in) for seam allowances at top and bottom.
For the piping fabric, use the width measurement of the skirt plus E plus seam allowances.

Violets

Just one and a quarter times fullness was used for this lined slipcover shade, which is pretty and feminine enough without being "frilly". The neat binding at the top sits perfectly on a plain card shade beneath and balances the frilled hem. Tiny piping just strengthens the violet tones in the flowers.

To make up

1 Following the chart on page 101, from the top fabric, cut two lengths for the skirt and lining, one for the top binding and one for the frill. From the piping fabric, cut enough to pipe the top and bottom edges of the shade. Make up the piping (see page 124). Join the short sides of the skirt, lining and frill fabrics to make three tubes. Press seams flat. To make up the frill, fold in half lengthwise, wrong sides together. Divide the length into ten equal sections and mark each with a coloured tack.

2 Stitch the skirt piping to the right side of the top fabric, along the hemline. Join neatly. Divide the hemline into ten equal sections and mark each with a coloured tack. Also mark these divisions along the top edge. Pin the frill over the piping,with raw edges matching and lining up the ten marked sections. Make equal pleats between the divisions, pinning them in place as you go (1). Stitch.

3 With right sides together, pin the lining over the frill. Keep the pins at right angles to the raw edges. Turn over and stitch together from the other side, so that you can follow the piping stitching line. Turn right side out, press and pin the two top raw edges together. Run a gathering thread through both layers, 1.5 cm (⅝ in) down from the raw edges. Draw up to fit the top of the under shade, spacing gathers evenly.

4 Stitch the top piping to the top edge of the gathered skirt (2) and neaten the join. Pin the self-binding over the piping. Overlap the short ends and turn back the upper raw edge. Stitch and trim seam to 1 cm (⅜ in). Fold the binding to the inside, pin (3) and slipstitch to the stitching line with small, neat stitches. Slip the finished cover over a plain shade.

1

2

3

YOU WILL NEED

- *card or fabric under shade*
- *top fabric, as chart on page 101*
- *same or contrast fabric for lining, as chart on page 101*
- *fabric for band*
- *approximately 20 buttons to decorate*
- *satin ribbon for bow*

MEASURE

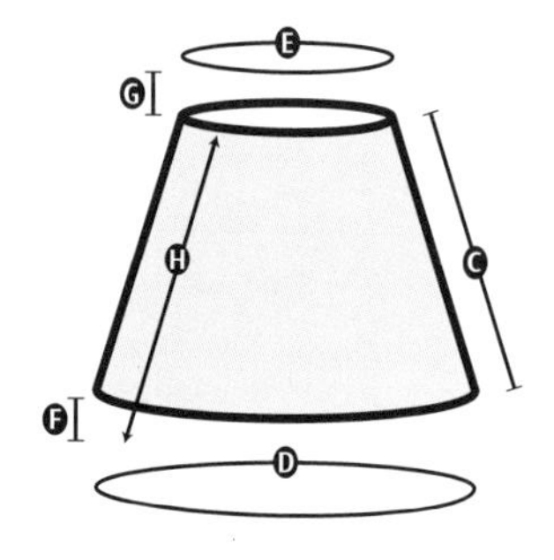

C = slope
D= base circumference
E = top circumference
F = hem allowance
G = frill allowance
H = lining and bottom band

For the top skirt depth, measure C + twice G + seam allowances, for the lining depth, measure C + F, which will give you H and add seam allowances, then use the chart on page 101 to find the fabric width for your shade.

Bordered hem

The skirts can be as full as you like on gathered shades, this one has barely more fullness than the circumference of the under shade, so that the bordered hem sits almost straight.

To make up

1 Cut out the top and lining fabrics. Join the short sides to make two tubes and press the seams open. Stitch the fabrics together along the hemline, right sides together. Open out and press the seam downwards. Measure 3.5 cm (1½ in) down from the seamline and press the lining to the back along this line.

2 Pin round the bottom and the top to hold the two layers firmly together. From the front, topstitch along the seam line, then again in a parallel line 1 cm (⅜ in) below. Topstitch along the fold line and again 1 cm (⅜ in) above.

3 Fold 4.5 cm (1¾ in) of the heading to the back to make the frill. Run two gathering threads round 3.5 cm (1½ in) from the top. Pull up, so that the cover fits comfortably over the under shade and secure the ends. Make a fabric band following the instructions on page 125 and slip stitch in place on the inside to hold the gathers in position and to conceal the raw edges. Finish with buttons round the bottom edge as shown. Tie the ribbon in a bow at the top.

Ruched heading

For a very simple heading, fold the top over to make a 1.5 cm (⅝ in) double hem. Top stitch 2 mm (1/12 in) from the top and again 2 mm (1/12 in) from the fold. At the front of the cover, make two neat buttonholes within the channel. Make up a fabric rouleau (see page 125) or cut a length of ribbon and thread through. Pull up to fit the top of the frame and tie into a bow.

Pleated heading

Instead of gathering the skirt, box or knife pleats can be used to control the fullness. Plan the pleats, pin in place - it's alright if they overlap a little - and stitch near to the raw edge to hold. Picot gimp covers the stitching line and holds the pleats in place at the top and creates a decorative border at the bottom.

Double layers

Two layers of skirts have more fullness and body than one, but only one layer should be lined, if any, or the fabric density prevents the light from shining through.

Finish the edges either with a ribbon stitched to cover the raw edges or fine piping and a small facing to enclose them.

To pipe the edges, use very fine cord to make the piping, then stitch to the hemline of the skirt. Cut 4 cm (1½ in) strips of the same fabric and stitch along the piping line to make a facing. Trim the seams, fold the facing to the back, press under the raw edge, then slip stitch to the skirt, catching single threads only and taking care not to pull the threads too tightly.

Pin and press the two layers together, measuring to keep the hemlines parallel.

Join together at the top by making a stand-up frill stitched in place with a band of the lining fabric (see page 125) or make a neat self-binding at the top (see page 125).

Butterfly edging

Butterfly edging strips can be made in contrasting or self fabric and hand stitched to a finished cover. Thread velvet or satin ribbon through for added interest. Follow the instructions on page 30 to make the edging, always keeping the width and pleat size equal and in proportion to the finished shade. Make the slipcover shade following the instructions on page 100.

Lined shades

Lined shades are attractive if the cover will be seen from beneath or if you want to turn the hem up into peaks. Cut the linings exactly the same size as the top skirt. Join the short sides of both to make two tubes. Finish the hemline with piping or binding. To pipe the hemline, stitch piping along the hemline on the right side of the main skirt. Pin the lining to the piping line, right sides together, then stitch just inside the previous stitching line. Turn right side out, press and pin the two layers together so that the headings are made up as if working with one piece.

To bind the hem, pin and press the two layers together, wrong sides together, and lining up the seams. Treat these two layers as one and add a strip of binding to the lower edge (see page 124).

Pintucks and pearls

Finish each pintuck with a small pearl bead or crystal drop for elegant simplicity.

Anyone who has watched historical dramas on big or small screen and has ended up paying more attention to the costumes than to the dialogue will be subject to the charms of pintucks and pearls. Being subjected to the working conditions of nineteenth century dressmakers would probably make us less romantic about the work that goes into fine decorative detail but in the comfort of our own homes, we can achieve similar effects without shattering any illusions.

What better way to light the clutter of a dressing table than with dainty silk shades? Never mind designer creations that spend 99 per cent of the time in wardrobes - here is made-to-measure, hand-crafted, fine needlework to be enjoyed every day. Crisp pintucks high-lighted by tiny beads give the lighting a delicate softness.

There is something hugely satisfying about these carefully planned and executed shades. They need not be confined to the bedroom, as the tailored look will add refinement to any room and will translate effectively to more masculine colours and materials. Imagine that your worktable has been transplanted to an atelier in the heyday of haute couture and create something special for your most important client - yourself!

Once you have mastered template making and pattern cutting for these shades, you will be able to progress to more and more imaginative designs. Silks and cottons are the easiest fabrics to start with, but why not experiment with velvets, wool felts, damasks and heavily textured fabrics for winter covers?

Remember that scale is an important consideration: pintucks should really be reserved for smaller shades, perhaps no larger than 40 cm (16 in) coolies or 35.5 cm (14 in) empires.

Use silks and taffetas either in a plain colour or with a tiny pattern. I have used organdie to face these fabrics because it is light enough not to make a ridge along the seamline when pressed, but has the character to add form and bounce to the hemline. Cotton fabric in a matching colour to the top fabric may be used for heavier fabrics and self lining for medium weight fabrics. If you prefer the hem to drop down rather than to bounce out, cut the hem several centimetres (one or two inches) longer and use a very soft cotton to line.

YOU WILL NEED

- *card or fabric under shade*
- *1 m (1 yd) calico or muslin for toile and template*
- *ruler*
- *1 m (1 yd) silk or taffetta*
- *small glass beads with holes, pearl or glass beads or sequins*
- *contrast marking thread*

Taffeta pintucks and pearls

Silk taffetta is really pleasing to work with as it responds freely to finger pressing and gentle scrunching to make interesting shapes. Tiny glass and pearl beads in tones of bronze, silver, sand and clear glass lift the creamy silk subtly and unobtrusively rather like the inside of an oyster shell.

To make up

1 Make a template for your shade in calico or tightly-woven fabric (see page 125) and divide into four sections.

2 Mark one piece into eight equal sections. Measure 10 - 15 cm (4 - 6 in) down the centre line from the top edge and mark with a pencil. Measure 5 - 8 cm (2 - 3 in) down the two outer edges and mark. Using a ruler, join up the mark on the lefthand edge with the centre mark and make a mark on the three remaining lines at the point where the ruler crosses them. Repeat on the righthand side (1).

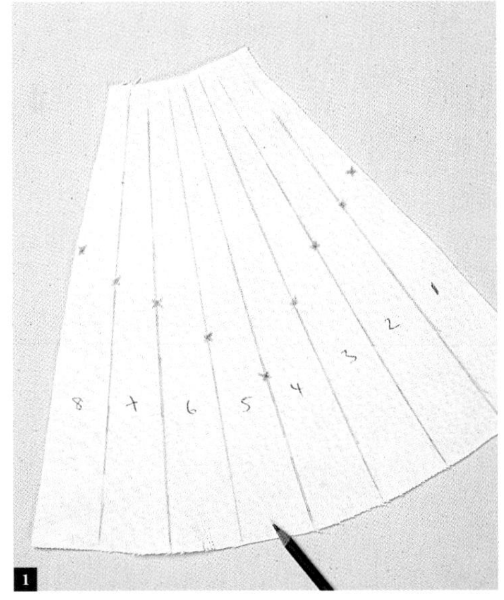

1

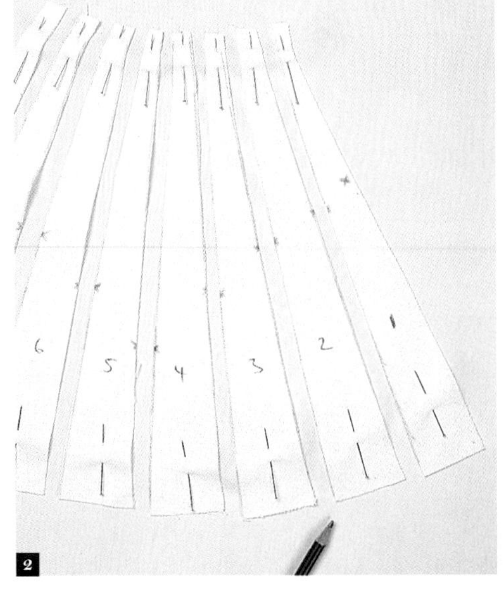

2

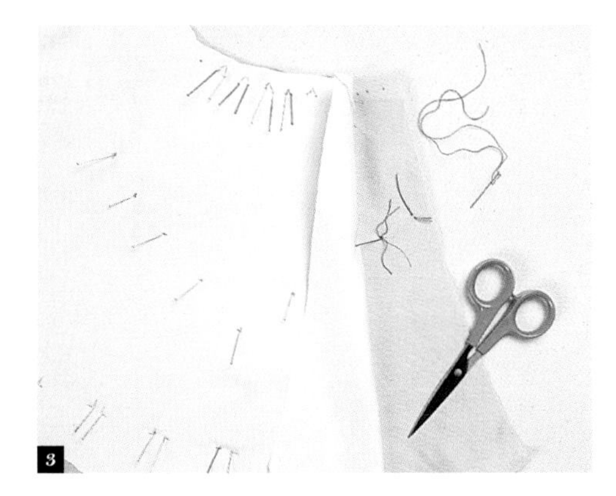

3 Now cut this piece into eight along the marked lines. Position the pieces onto the toile fabric leaving 1 cm (3/8 in) gaps for the tucks between (2). Transfer the pencil marks and make new ones at the top and bottom of each section.

4 Fold this piece over three times to make the whole shade and mark each section up to match the first. Add 1.5 cm (5/8 in) all round for the seam allowances. Cut out the calico toile. Place this pattern onto the top fabric and transfer all pencil marks with marking tacks (3), then cut out.

5 With wrong sides together, stitch the tucks between tacks. Join the short sides with a tiny French seam. Using the toile as a pattern, cut a hem facing 8 cm (3¼ in) deep from the lining fabric (see page 123). Neaten the inner edge. Pin the hems, right sides together and stitch, taking a 1.5 cm (5/8 in) seam. Trim the seam to 0.5 cm (¼ in). Press the facing to the back, turn under the raw edge, join the side edges and pin in place.

6 Bind the top following the instructions on page 125, using a strip of fabric cut on the cross 5 cm (2 in) wide.

7 Hand stitch pearls or beads to the end of each tuck (4) and beads or sequins at random round the skirt. Use these stitches to hold the facing in place (5).

This fabric shade (right) is past its sell-by date and therefore an excellent candidate for a new slipcover, such as the one shown opposite.

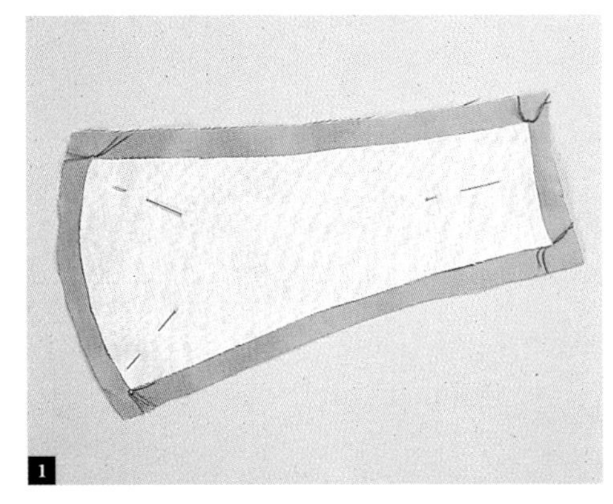

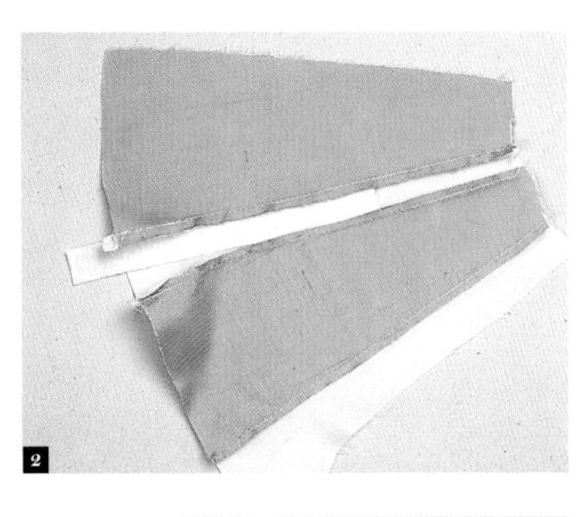

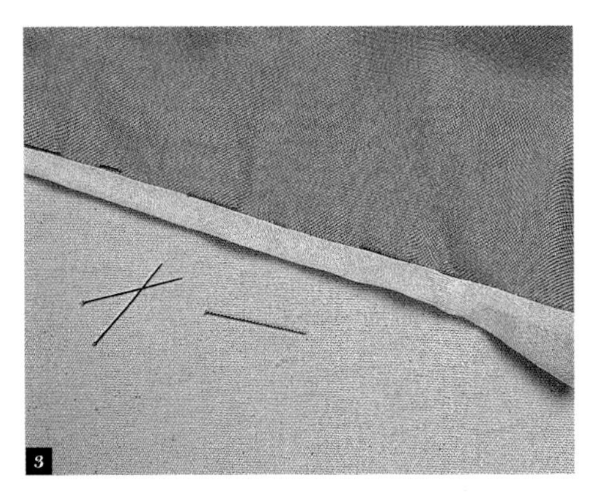

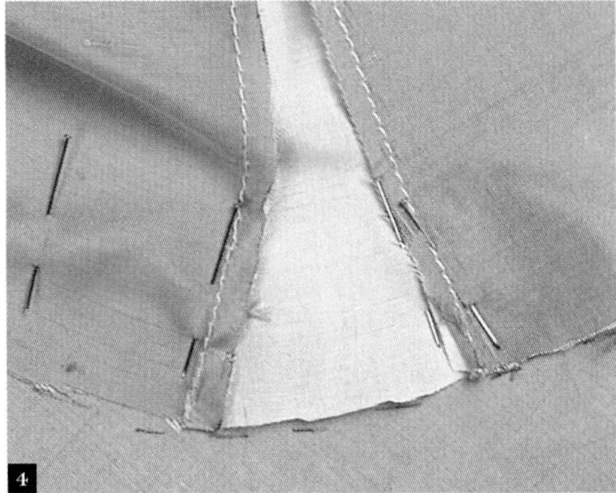

YOU WILL NEED

- *card or fabric under shade*
- *calico or tightly woven fabric for the template*
- *fabrics A and B, see method*
- *self-coloured lining or organdie to face hem*

MEASURE

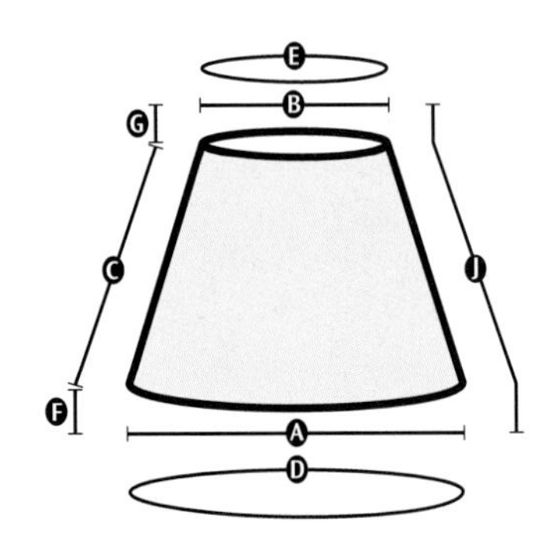

C = slope
F = hem allowance

Measure the slope of your under shade and make a template for the contrast pintucks following the shape below.

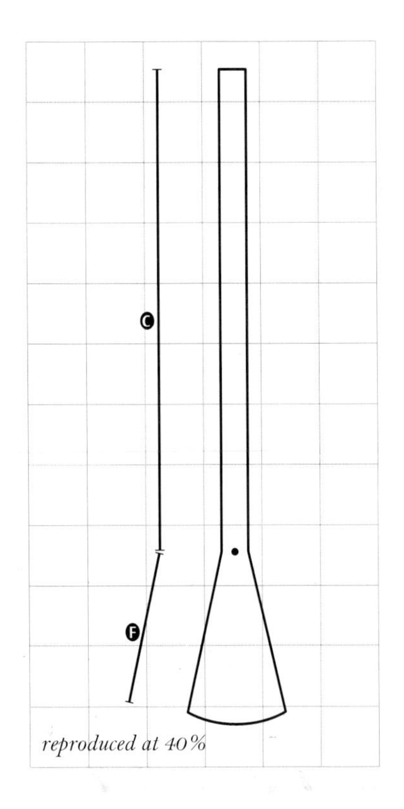

reproduced at 40%

Contrast pintucks

The careful shaping of the sections and tucks gives a gently undulating border to these close-fitting slipcover shades.

To make up

1 Make a template for your shade in calico or tightly-woven fabric (see page 125).

2 Divide this into ten sections and work with one of these. Add 5.5 cm (2¼ in) to the bottom. Cut another toile section incorporating this allowance.

3 Using this piece as a pattern, cut out ten pieces in fabric A (1), adding 1.5 cm (⅝ in) seam allowances all round. From fabric B cut ten tucks using the template provided, adapting C to the slope of your under shade and adding 1.5 cm (⅝ in) seam allowances all round.

4 Join all pieces together from the bottom to the top, pinning sections and tucks alternately. Stitch together, taking up the 1.5 cm (⅝ in) seam allowance. Cut a strip of fabric 2 cm (¾ in) wide and place onto each "tuck", underneath the seam. Press seams over this strip to prevent the seams making ridges on the front of the fabric (2). Trim the seams.

5 Fold the tucks in half, right sides together, enclosing seams. Stitch on the stitching lines from small dot to top. Always stitch in the same direction (3).

6 Make the hem facing (4) with a strip of fabric A 7 cm (2¾ in) deep and to the length of the circumference of the lower edge of the finished cover plus 3 cm (1¼ in), see page 123. Press 0.5 cm (¼ in) to the wrong side along one long side and stitch down. Pin the opposite side to the bottom of the cover, right sides together, and aligning raw edges. Stitch, taking the usual seam allowance. Trim seam to 0.5 cm (¼ in). Press to the inside, join the short sides and slip stitch to each tuck seam.

7 Bind the heading with a strip of either fabric A or B, 5 cm (2 in) wide following the instructions on page 125.

YOU WILL NEED

- *card or fabric under shade: suitable sizes are empire: 25 x 12.5 x 18 cm (10 x 5 x 7 in) and 30 x 15 x 20 cm (12 x 6 x 8 in) or coolie: 20 x 7.5 x 14 cm (8 x 3 x 5½ in), 25 x 7.5 x 16.5 cm (10 x 3 x 6½ in) and 30 x 10 x 18 cm (12 x 4 x 7 in). These will take 60 cm - 1 m (¾ - 1¼ yds) of fabric, plus extra for facing and top binding*
- *contrast marking thread*
- *calico or tightly woven fabric to make toile and template*
- *top fabric, see above*
- *organdie for facing*
- *20 pearl drops or beads*

Full length pintucks

These tailored silk slipcover shades fit snugly over a coolie or empire under shade with a softly ruffled edge standing out just beneath it.

To make up

1 Make a template for your shade from calico or any offcut of tightly woven fabric, as described on page 125.

2 Divide into twenty equal sections and number consecutively, then cut into twenty pieces.

3 Place the pieces onto another piece of calico leaving 1.5 cm (⅝ in) gaps between each. Keep the top and bottom circles flowing evenly. Mark seam allowances of 1.5 cm (⅝ in) at each side, 1.5 cm (⅝ in) at the top and 8.5 cm (3½ in) at the lower edge. Mark each corner of each template piece with marking tacks. Remove the templates.

4 Place this new calico pattern onto your top fabric and cut out. Transfer the marking tacks. Make tucks by joining the marking tacks, right sides together, and tacking together, then tack the two short sides of the shade together. Sit over the card shade to check the fit and adjust as necessary.

5 Hand or machine stitch the tucks in place and press down. For a neat finish, take the threads inside at the bottom of the pintucks and knot or make a double stitch inside.

6 To make the facing, cut a strip of organdie 9 cm (3¾ in) deep and the length of the circumference of the hem plus 3 cm (1¼ in). Press under 0.5 cm (¼ in) to the wrong side of one long side and stitch down. Stitch the facing to the hem, right sides together, taking a 1.5 cm (⅝ in) seam allowance. Trim back to 0.5 cm (¼ in), press to the back and slip stitch to the bottom of each tuck.

7 Bind the top of the shade with self or contrast fabric cut on the cross 5 cm (2 in) wide, and following the instructions on page 125. Stitch pearl drops or beads at the base of each pintuck.

Hand-printed shot taffeta (opposite) is such a premium fabric that I could not bear to cut it, instead, I draped it over a shade and pintucked it to fit. The first tucks were pinned from the top to the base rings of the shade at the four points of the compass, then at north-east, north-west, south-east and south-west and again in between until the fabric sat comfortably against the under shade. The top of the shade was bound and the little fullness which accumulated stitched into a natty twist.

Winter Warmers

To completely furnish a country house or weekend retreat, to make winter slipcovers for tables, sofas, chairs and lampshades, the subtle blending of country fabrics with sophisticated silks and velvets has never before been as acceptable, as inspirational - or as challenging. This cover is made in the same way as the one on page 119 but it is cut deeper and the bottom has been frayed and scalloped.

Imagine a cosy winter evening by an open fire: you sit idly toasting crumpets, an oil lamp glows on a side table, a candle flickers on the windowsill... How soothing the low light is - it almost makes the cold of winter worthwhile! Our real homes, however, have electric light that, although safe and reliable, is usually so harsh that the comforting effect of any amount of atmospheric decor is obliterated.

You may not want to curl up in an armchair every evening but it is possible to create a snug atmosphere by slipping a winter warmer of a lampshade over the usual one. If low-level lighting is required, heavy weaves, wools, tartans or felts can be used, red fabrics make a good substitute for candlelight. Velvet is perfect for creating intimate pools of light while lending its own tactile warmth to the room.

Black might seem a strange colour for a shade but very dark colours can be used to create a spotlight effect on a special ornament or display. Dark, dense fabric is suitable for slipcovers to be thrown over pale under shades in the evening. Velvet is an especially good-tempered fabric for rolling up and storing when the slipcover shade is not in use.

When choosing trimmings, look for metal or leather buttons, wooden beads or even small pieces of coloured glass to complement the substantial fabrics that you are using.

YOU WILL NEED

- *card or fabric under shade*
- *top fabric, see method*
- *embroidery thread or 4 ply wool*
- *buttons, beads or sequins to decorate*
- *leather or complementary fabric, for binding top and bottom*

Winter colours

It's good fun to make winter covers which slip over creamy silk fabric shades or card under shades. Reds, browns and corals filter light warmly but greens and browns will give a cold, unfavourable light. Choose fabrics which will allow some light to pass through, especially for important lamps. For side lights, the fabric can almost be a blackout, allowing directional light.

The universal appeal of wools, tartans and plaids never seems to wane (right). And especially over the last decade the influence of some fashion designers on home furnishings has led to the exciting and imaginative teaming of floral cottons and linens with country tweeds, chunky knits and Scottish plaids in infinite colour combinations.

Make a template (see page 125) to fit your shade and divide into six sections. Cut fabric sections plus seam allowances. Stitch together, then bind the top and bottom (see page 124) with leather or other suitable material. Jacket buttons stitched down the seams lines carry through the country tweed theme.

The specific qualities of very dark colours are often useful in a particular situation as in the black velvet shown here (*left*). Light is not able to diffuse through the sides, so it falls in generous pools onto the surface below. This spotlight effect can be used imaginatively to highlight a special object or display. Eminently suitable for evening use, a slipcover shade can be thrown over to darken the light from a pale under shade.

Make up this shade following the instructions for gathered shades in the Summer Garden chapter on page 100, keeping the fullness to a maximum of one and a half times the base circumference for these heavier fabrics.

YOU WILL NEED

- *stretched under shade*
- *calico for template*
- *felt, see method*
- *stencil acetate or a bought stencil*
- *gold spray*

MEASURE

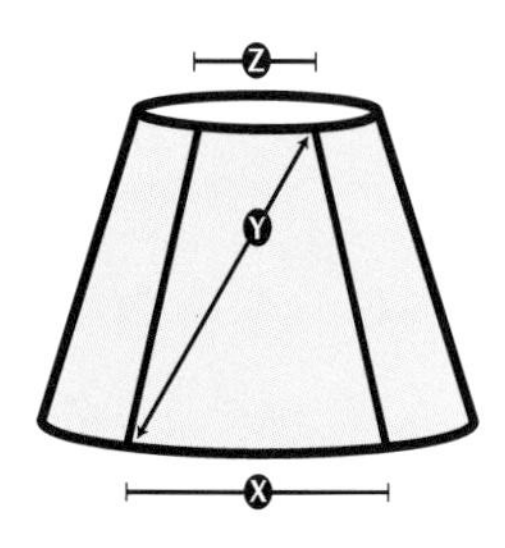

X = base of one section
Y = diagonal
Z = top of one section

Measure one section and cut a piece of calico roughly to this shape.

Instead of a stencilled design, you could paste or appliqué motifs or use a sharp hole punch to make punched patterns (far right). Try combining fabrics for double or multicoloured panels and pipe or bind the seams with a contrasting colour.

Quick felt slip cover

Felt is such a good tempered fabric to work with - no hemming or finishing needed - that it is perfect for a simple cover to slip over a stretched shade to change the atmosphere for an evening or a season. Use the rose stencil below placed randomly all over the shade and spray with gold paint, or make your own design.

(reproduced at 50%)

To make up

1 First make a template of one of the sections of the stretched undershade. To do this, take a piece of calico and pin to the top and bottom of the frame, then along the struts. Have a look at the instructions on page 12 for stretching. As this is a slipcover, the seams need to fit well but the top and bottom will not be held in place. Mark the seams with a light pencil. Trim away any excess fabric, leaving just 1 cm (⅜ in) seam allowances. Repeat with the other sections.

2 Remove the calico from the frame and cut pieces of felt to match, but making the top and bottom 3 cm (1¼ in) longer. Cut the edges into decorative scallops. Stencil each panel at this stage if you are using a centralised motif.

3 Stitch the sections, with right sides together and taking 1 cm (⅜ in) seam allowances. Tidy up the edges and stencil now if the design is randomly spaced over the whole shade, for example, if you are using the rose stencil.

FANTAISIE .. SONATE
Pour le Forte-Piano
THERESE de TRATTNERN
MOZART.
SEI
QUARTETTI
PER DUE VIOLINI VIOLA E VIOLONCELLO
Composti e Dedicati
al Signor
GIUSEPPE HAYDN
Maestro di Capella di S.A.
il Principe d'Esterhazy &c &c
Dal Suo Amico
W.A.MOZART
Opera X

Basic Techniques

SAFETY

Safety is the primary criterion for all things electrical. Make sure that every lamp is safe, and be especially aware of potential danger from the child's view-point.

The two most common causes of fire from side lamps are i) where a shade has been allowed to come into direct contact with the bulb and ii) faulty wiring and/or worn fittings.

1. Select products which have passed your country's safety regulations.
2. Don't buy cheap imports - or re-wire if you do.
3. Always renew fittings if you are using an antique base.
4. Replace worn fittings to make sure that a shade cannot be accidentally pushed to one side.
5. Keep flexes short or taped down so that no one can accidentally trip and a small child is not tempted to pull them.
6. Use only moulded plugs on portable lamps.
7. On/off switches should be independent of the plug and socket.
8. On/off switches must be within easy reach of a sitting or reclining position.
9. Never exceed the recommended bulb wattage for each shade size.
10. Always use candle bulbs for small shades - make sure that bulb and fabric never touch.
11. Make sure the shade to base ratio is balanced - lamps with top-heavy shades can be very easily overturned.
12. Not all candles are made to take the weight of a candle shade and fitting and many will bend under the weight - check before you purchase.
13. Never leave candles alight when you are out of the room.
14. Avoid table lamps in nurseries or guest rooms, which might be knocked over. Use wall fittings of the "Billy Baldwin" style with extending arms.
15. Never put lamps where the opening of a room or cupboard door might knock them over.
16. Never fit wall lights near curtains which might blow onto the fitting in a breeze.
17. Work areas need to be provided with more than adequate light. Don't make do with a table light when you really need a standard one.

PREPARING THE FRAME

* You will need: white enamel or household gloss paint, a small brush, fine gauge sandpaper or a sanding block and 1.5 cm (⅝ in) cotton tape.
* Most lampshade frames are plastic coated, so you will only need to tape the top and base rings and any struts which you will need to pin or stitch into.
* Check the frame carefully for any holes and fill these with white enamel or gloss paint.
* Rub down any sharp edges: use fine gauge paper or a sanding block.

To bind the frame

Successful binding requires you to keep the tape as taut as you possibly can, otherwise any fabric that you stitch to it will sag as the binding slips round the frame. Overlap each twist, so that there are only ever two layers of tape.

1. Begin with the top of the shade uppermost and one strut facing you. Rest the base of the shade on a table top or on your lap. Cut off a length of tape three times the length to be bound. Roll the tape into a ball and keep it in the palm of your hand, so that you are in control of the unwieldy lengths.
2. Start at the top of the strut, holding and twisting the tape as shown.

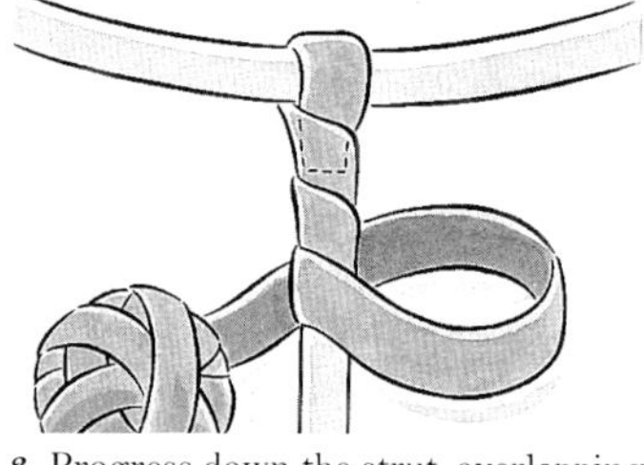

3. Progress down the strut, overlapping each twist halfway over the last one. Keep one finger on the last twist and pull tight, twist the tape and slip your finger down to hold this one as you pull tight and prepare for the next twist.
4. Finish the end of the strut with a loop. Pull tight and make a double stitch through the layers of tape to secure.

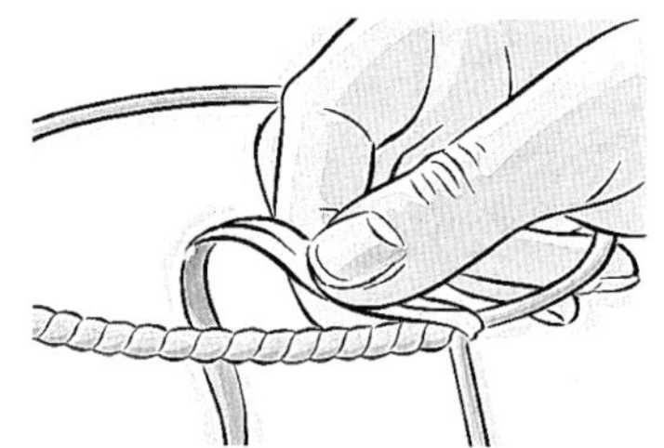

5. Once the struts have been bound, bind the top and base rings, starting the tape off as before. At each strut make a figure of eight with the tape to keep a tidy finish.

LININGS

Linings give a professional finish to a shade: the raw edges of the top cover are covered by the lining and the raw edges of the lining by the self-binding or braiding chosen to finish.
* Fabric linings can either be fitted inside the frame, so concealing the struts, or tight to the top of the frame, beneath the top cover.
* Lining fabrics should be stretchy so choose wool or silk crêpe.
* Choose a lightweight fabric to allow the maximum light to filter through.
* Cream or off-white colours give good, warm light.
* White linings might be needed for white shades but otherwise avoid white as it gives off a cold light.
* Coloured linings can be interesting. Try gold under rose pink; rich gold under buttermilk or antique gold under parchment for an "aged" look.
* Always use thread of the same fibre content - cotton with cotton and silk with wool or silk to stitch linings.

To make a pleated lining

1. Cut a rectangle of lining on the cross, equal in length to the circumference of the base ring, plus seam allowance and as deep as the frame plus 5 cm (2 in).
2. Join the short sides with a French seam.
3. Pin the lining to the base ring of the prepared frame, pinning the lining onto the front of the ring.

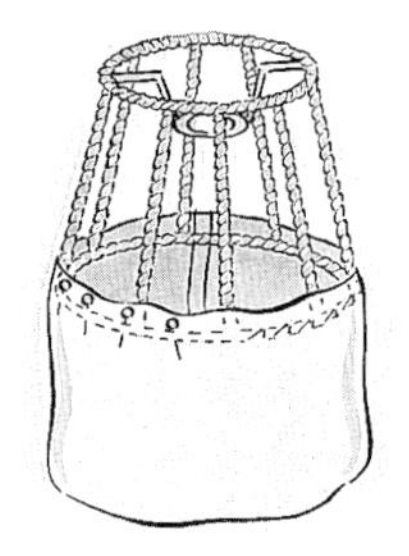

4. Stitch round the base ring securely using lampshades stitches 1.5 cm (⅝ in) in length (see next page).

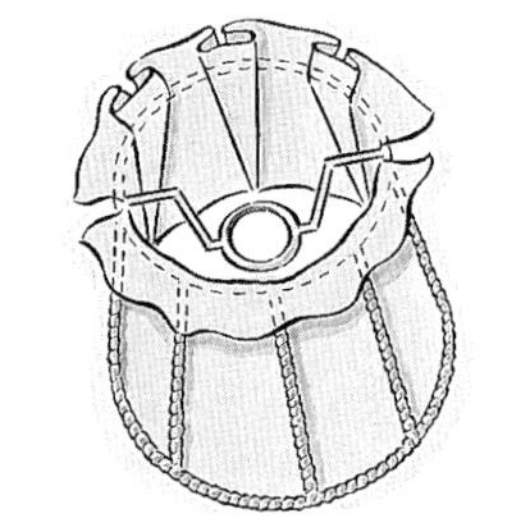

5. Pull the lining up inside the frame. Pull it up straight at each strut and pin to the top ring. Snip into the lining round the gimbal fitting, so that it can lie flat.
6. At each strut, pleat away the fullness. Make sure that the pleats are neat and even, since when the light is on any fold line becomes visible. The smaller the top ring in proportion to the base ring, the more fullness there will be to accommodate.
7. Re-pin the lining to the front of the frame, stretching it to its limit. Leave overnight to rest and if the lining has sagged, re-pin. Stitch in place once the fabric has remained taut for a period of time. Snip at each gimbal strut, so that the lining can be pulled up tightly. Stitch tightly and trim close to the stitching line.
8. Cut two pieces of lining fabric, 3 x 7 cm (1¼ x 2¾ in). Press into three lengthwise and fold round the gimbal fittings to conceal the cut edges. Stitch to the frame, then trim the excess fabric. The ends will be covered by the frame binding.

To make a tight lining

1. Once the frame has been prepared and before fitting the outer cover, cut two pieces of lining, on the cross, each enough for half of the frame.

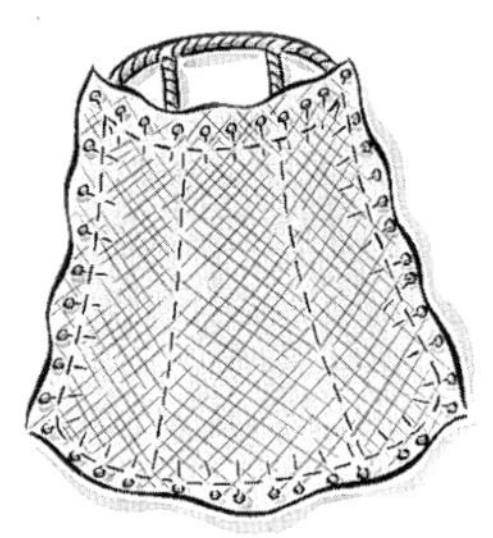

2. Pin one half to the frame at the four corners, then every 5 - 6 cm (2 - 2¼ in) between, working in a clockwise direction. The lining fabric must be taut, so keep pinning, stretching and re-pinning until there are no bubbles or pulls remaining. Most problems can be resolved by re-pinning diagonally opposite pairs of pins.
3. Pin the other half of the lining in the same manner, then pin the two pieces together at the sides.
4. Pencil mark round the frame top, base and side struts. Mark the top and bottom of each side seam with tacks. Trim the lining to 2 cm (¾ in) all round.

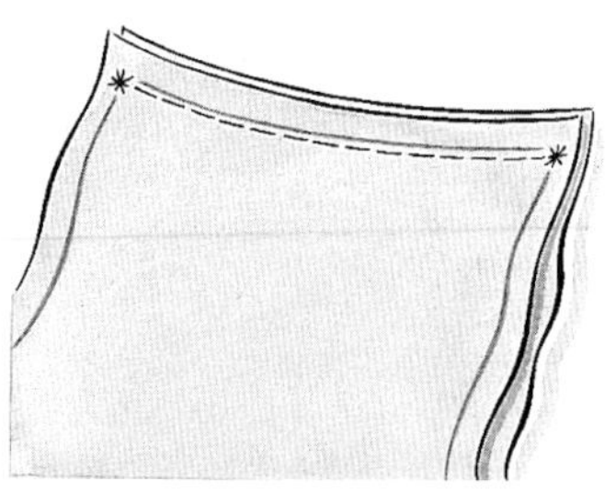

5. Remove the lining. Stitch the side seams, right sides together, just 2 mm (1/12 in) inside the pinned line - as the inside of the frame will be slightly smaller than the outside. Fit the lining loosely inside the frame to check the fit and, if necessary, stitch again just inside the last line of stitching. Trim the seam back neatly to just under 0.5 cm (¼ in). It is most important that this cut is not ragged or it will look really ugly when the lamp is on.

6. Keep the lining to one side as tight linings are almost always fitted after the top cover.

FACINGS

It is not always practical or advisable to line lampshade covers, simply because an extra layer of fabric further reduces the lamplight. But if the hem is finished with lace or piping, or left plain, a facing will be needed to enclose the raw edges.

* Very fine fabrics, such as organza, organdie and cotton lawn, are useful, preferably in a colour to match the main fabric. Facings need to be cut from the final toile (fabric pattern) once all seam allowances have been incorporated.

1. Open up one seam of the finished toile and lay it flat onto the facing fabric. Draw round the hemline, and along the opened seam for 6 - 8 cm (2½ - 2¾ in).

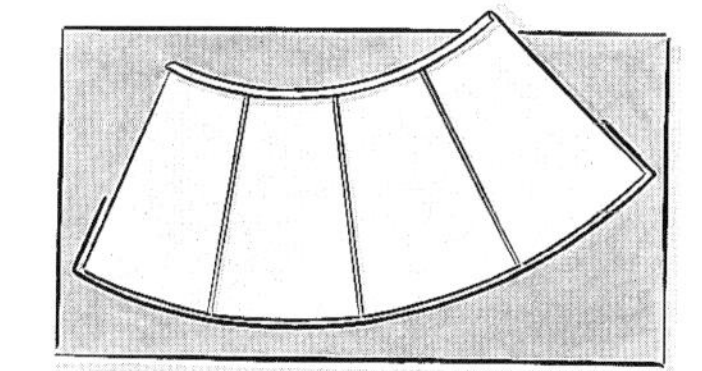

2. Remove the toile and draw another line 6 - 8 cm (2½ - 2¾ in) away from the pencilled line and parallel to it to mark the inner edge and cut out. Turn under 0.5 cm (¼ in) of the inner edge and stitch close to the fold line to neaten.

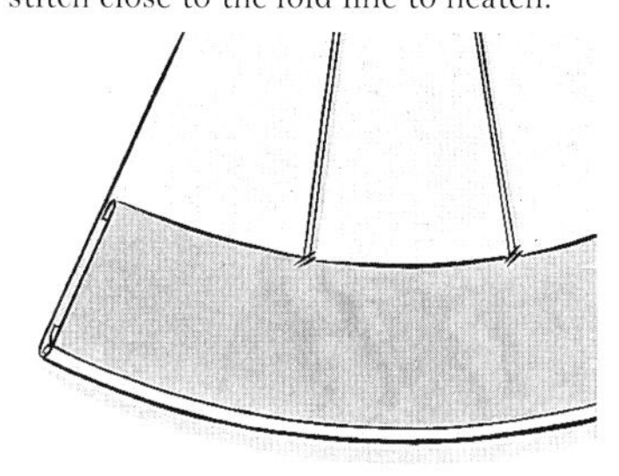

3. Pin the facing to the main fabric, right sides together and stitch along the hemline. Trim the seam to 0.5 cm (¼ in). Press the seam to one side and press the facing to the back. Slip stitch the side seams and slip stitch the facing to any available seams or tucks to hold in place. It is usually not necessary to stitch the whole facing down and better not to emphasise its presence with a ridge caused by stitching.

STITCHES

Cut thread lengths which are manageable - no more than 50 cm (20 in) in length and using double thread where strength is important and single thread where invisibility is the priority.

* Start and finish with a double stitch, hiding it inside the hem; knots can be bulky and likely to unravel.

Hemming stitch

A neat "weaving" hemstitch which is all but invisible.

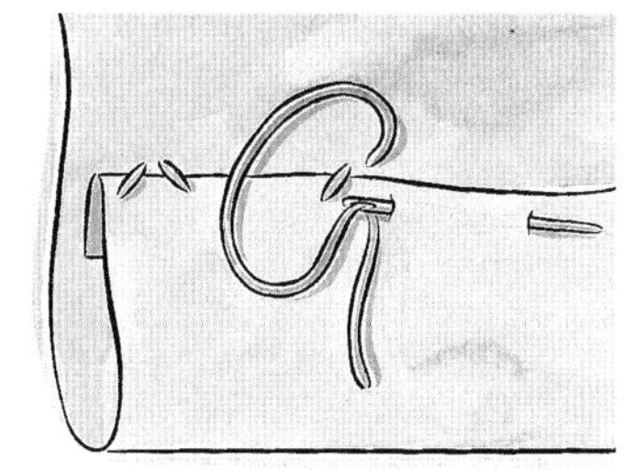

Slide the needle along the folded hem for approximately 1.5 cm (⅝ in), bring it out and pick up two threads of the main fabric and push the needle straight back into the fold.

Herringbone stitch

Herringbone stitch neatly finishes any raw edge which will later be covered by a second layer of fabric or lining.

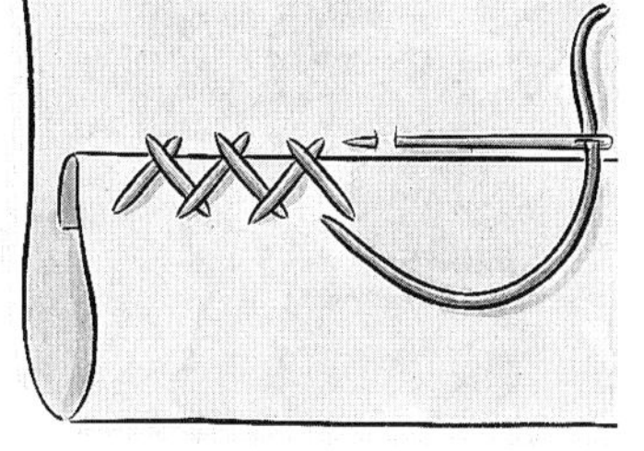

Work from left to right for right handers and right to left for left handers, with the hem facing you. Stitch into the hem taking up about four threads, take the needle to the right keeping the thread to the right of the needle and pick up a couple of threads from the main fabric. Take the needle to the right, again keeping the thread to the right and pick up three - four threads from the hem. These stitches should be 1 - 1.5 cm (⅜ - ⅝ in) wide and deep.

Lampshade stitch

A strong stitch always worked with double thread to hold fabric securely to the lampshade frame.

Make a double stitch at right angles to the raw edge. Bring the thread diagonally across for 1.5 cm (⅝ in) and make another double stitch at right angles. Keep the thread taut.

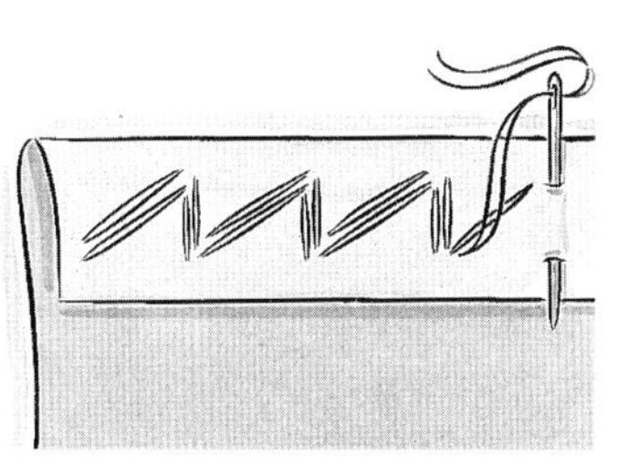

Blanket stitch

A decorative and practical edging to neaten the raw edge of a heavy fabric or folded edge of a medium weight cloth.

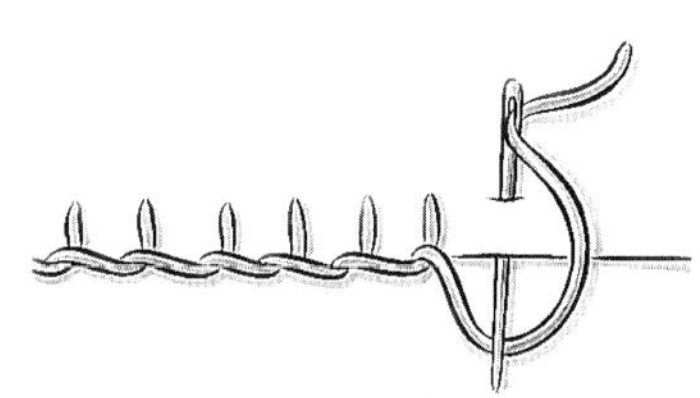

Secure the thread and start at the edge. Keeping the thread in one hand push the needle through the cloth from front to back, approximately 1 cm (⅜ in) from the edge. Bring the needle up through the loose thread to make a loop and pull gently to make the stitch. Again holding the thread with one hand, push the needle through the cloth in the same direction, 1 cm (⅜ in) from the last stitch. Make the loop and pull to tighten.

Buttonhole stitch

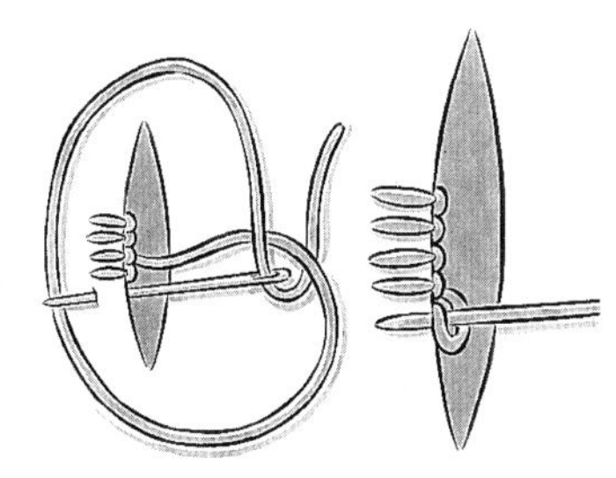

Starting at the cut edge, push the needle through the cloth from back to front approximately 3 mm (⅛ in) from the edge. Twist the thread round the needle as shown and pull the needle through. Tighten gently to make a knot which exactly covers the raw edge. As you continue, keeping the stitches close together, these knots will make a ridge along the cut edge with no threat of fraying.

PINNING

It is important to pin two layers of fabric together in such a way that they will not slip when stitched.

1. Firstly, place one layer of fabric flat on the worktable. Lay the top layer over loosely so that neither edge is being stretched. Start by securing with one pin at each end and one in the centre, with pins parallel to the raw edge. Pin the two fabrics along their length at approximately 15 cm (6 in) intervals, then twice in between these. You will need to take out each pin as soon as the machine foot approaches, so remember to position all in same direction, with the heads facing you when the seam allowance is on the right.

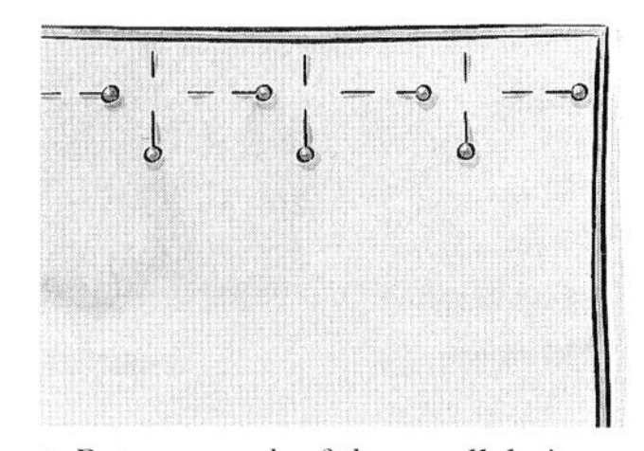

2. Between each of the parallel pins, position another pin at right angles. These are restraining pins which will be left in the fabric until stitching is completed, so make sure that the pin penetrates the fabric equally on either side of the seam allowance. Most machines will run straight over them, but if you have trouble, then just stitch very slowly, removing each pin at the last moment.

Pinning gathered fabric

When pinning gathered fabric to a flat piece, place the flat piece on the table and lay the gathered fabric over the top with raw edges towards you. Match the marking tacks, spreading the gathers evenly between and pin at right angles to the raw edges with pins 1 - 1.5 cm (⅜ - ⅝ in) apart, keeping each gather straight and even. Each pin should penetrate the fabric on either side of the seam line, so that they can remain in place while you stitch over them. Pin parallel to the raw edges, away from the seam line, not as a line to follow but just to hold the gathers down. Remove all pins and gathering thread once the seam has been stitched.

PIPING

Choose your piping cord according to the project. Nos 00 and 01 are the most suitable to finish a gathered hem but any size can be used for decorative effect. Just remember that the larger the piping, the stiffer the hemline will become. If in doubt, make a test piece.

* Cut lengths of fabric for piping on the straight if there are no curved edges to be piped and on the cross (at an angle of 45° across the grain) if you want the piping to fit round scallops, points, etc.

* Keep lengths as long as possible. For lampshades there should be no need for any more than one join. As a general

rule, cut strips 4.5 cm (1¾ in) wide but your might prefer to test first.

* Wrap a piece of fabric round the piping, pin close to the piping and allow 1.5 cm (⅝ in) seam allowance on either side.

* Fold the piping strip in half round the cord and machine close to the the cord.

Pinning piping

Always pin so that the raw edges of the piping line up with those of the top fabric.

* To pipe round curves, snip into the seam allowance of the piping at 1 - 1.5 cm (⅜ - ⅝ in) intervals from the edge right up to the stitching line. Pin along the stitching line and at right angles from just behind the cord.

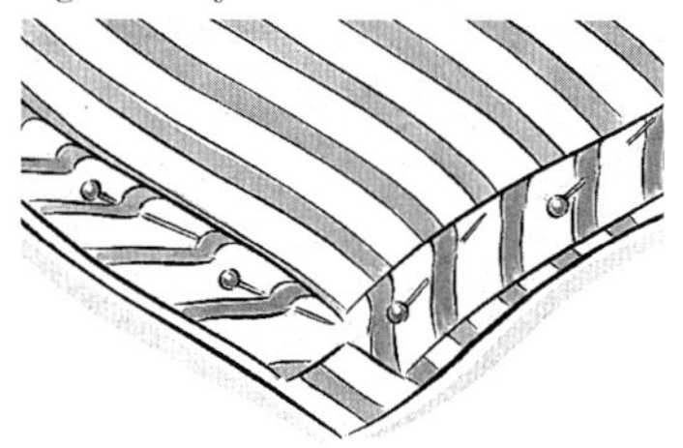

* To pipe round a right angle, snip sharply into the corner, then bend the cord firmly to sit along the seam allowance.

Joining piping

Leave approximately 6 cm (2½ in) extra at the start and finish. Unpick the casing for 5 cm (2 in) on one side and cut away the cord so that both ends butt up. Trim the fabric end to 45° and press under 1 cm (⅜ in). Sleeve this end over the other and pin securely in place before stitching.

SEAMS

Pressing

When pressing seams always insert a strip of fine to medium weight cotton between the seam and the top fabric to prevent any ridges forming on the front.

Flat seam

Pin two fabrics right sides together (see pinning) and stitch along the seam allowance given - usually 1.5 cm (⅝ in). Press the seam flat.

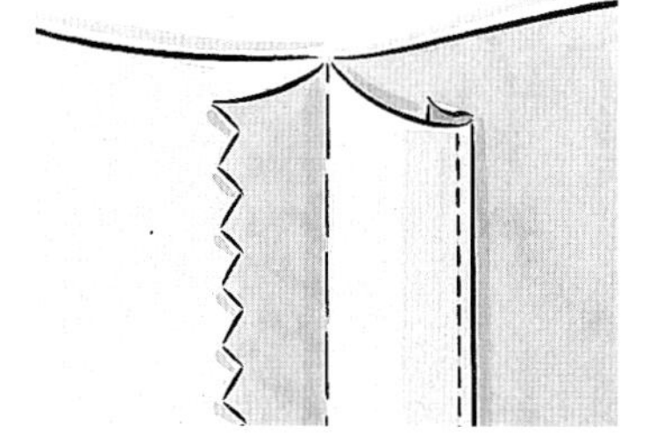

Leave the raw edges unfinished if the shade will have a lining. If not, neaten with an overlocking machine, pink the edge or press 0.5 cm (¼ in) under each side and hand or machine stitch close to the fold.

French seam

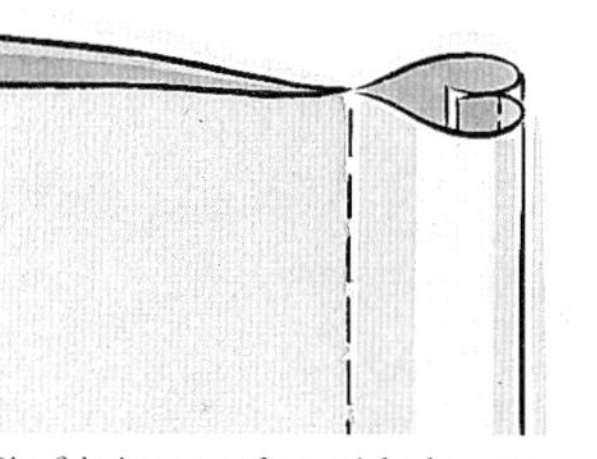

Pin fabrics together with the wrong sides facing. Stitch a seam of no more than 0.5 cm (¼ in). Trim back to 0.25 cm (⅛ in) for fine fabrics and press to one side. Pin another seam, with right sides together, enclosing the first within it and stitch as close as possible to the raw edges. Press.

HEMS

Standard double folded hems are too bulky and uninteresting to finish off the bottom of most lampshades.

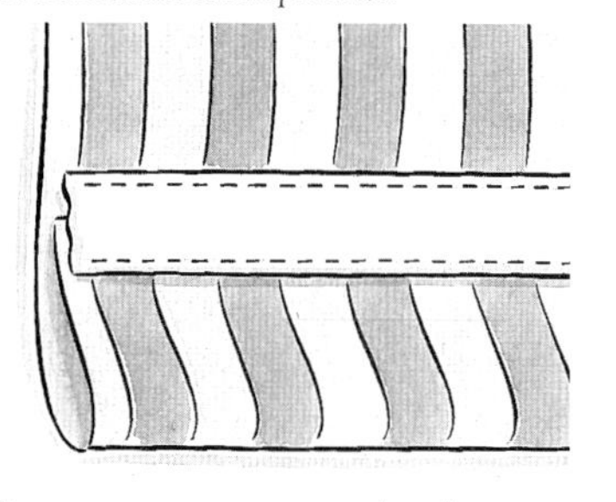

A neat way to cover raw edges is to use ribbon. Press the hem allowance (usually 1.5 cm/⅝ in) to the front of the skirt. Pin ribbon over, with the pins at right angles. Join the ribbon ends by folding under one end to overlap the other. Topstitch the ribbon just 2 mm (1/12 in) from each edge.

If the fabric is reversible, you could set the ribbon up from the hem. If not, make the bottom edge of the ribbon the hemline. Almost any ribbon in any width can be used as long as the weights of the fabric and the ribbon are compatible.

Shell hemming

Shell hemming is a neat and quick finish. Roll a double hem to just 0.7 cm (5/16 in) and pin (rather than pressing).

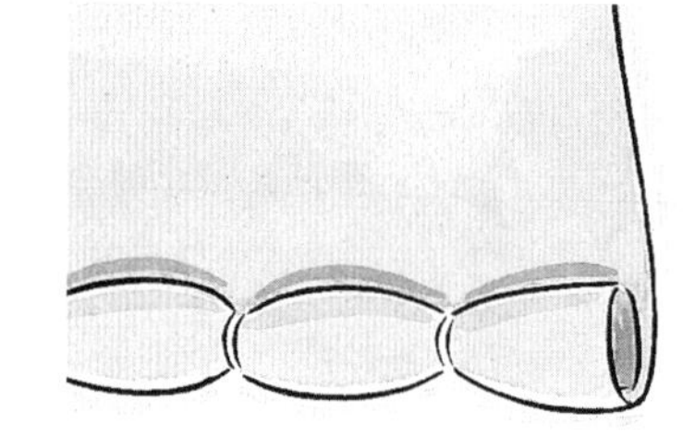

Using matching thread, make a double stitch at right angles to the hem, finishing 0.7 cm (5/16 in) in from the edge. Slide the needle along the fold for 1.5 - 2 cm (⅝ - ¾ in) and make a small stitch on the inside to secure. To make the "shell" shape, take the thread round the hem, then push the needle straight through from front to back. Pull tight. Repeat, then slide the needle along the fold for 1.5 - 2 cm (⅝ - ¾ in) to the next stitch.

BINDING

Cut binding strips on the cross (45°), if they are to be used round curves, scallops or points and on the straight, if to be used straight. Each should be cut four times the finished width required.

* Try to cut lengths which are long enough without joins, but if joins are inevitable, then the seam must be on the cross to reduce bulk when the whole is folded into four.

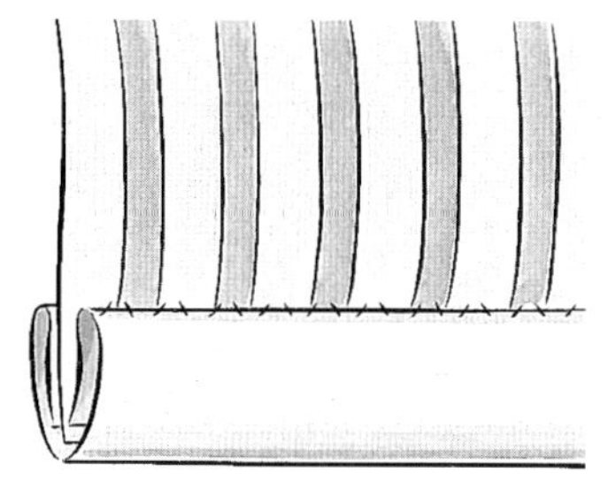

If the binding is to be 1.5 cm (⅝ in) finished width, then the strip will be cut 6 cm (2½ in) wide.

* Pin the binding (see pinning) to the top fabric and stitch 1.5 cm (⅝ in) from the raw edge. Press the binding away from the top fabric, pressing the seam line as flat as possible. Fold the binding under, and pin, measuring to make sure the binding remains the same width all along.

* Press, avoiding the pins. From the back fold the raw edge under so that the binding width at the back is exactly that at the front and the fold line just covers the stitching line. Pin, press and hem stitch along the fold, picking up threads from the stitching line.

Binding a corner

Pin and stitch the first section of binding in place, stopping short of the corner by the finished width of the binding.

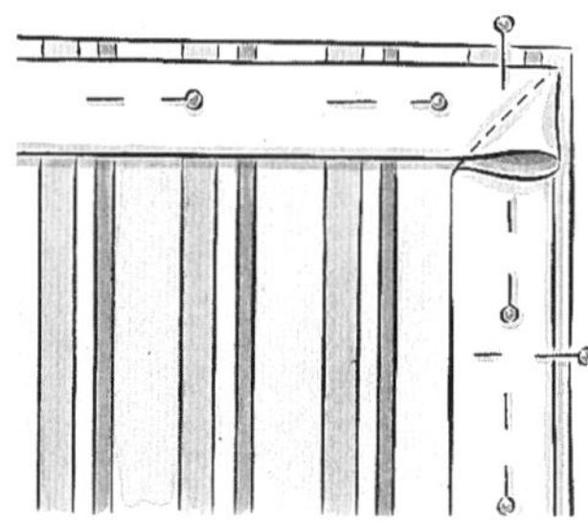

1. Fold the binding back on itself and pin down. Pin along to the next corner. Insert the needle the width of the binding from both sides of the corner - this should be exactly next to the last stitch underneath the flap and continue to stitch the next section along the seam allowance.

2. Press the binding away from the top fabric and mitre the corner. Fold the binding over to the required width, press and pin.

3. Turn to the back and fold the binding in half to conceal the raw edge with the fold line against the stitching line. Mitre each corner in the opposite direction, snipping along the fold line on one side to allow the mitre to lie flat.

FRILLED HEADINGS

If a shade or shade cover is not fitted to a frame there will be fullness at the top which needs to be taken up. Gathering into a plain binding or ribbon "collar" is an option, as is gathering to make a frilled heading.

* A short frilled heading of 2 cm (¾ in) will make a neat "stand up" heading, a deeper frill of 6 cm (2½ in) can be fashioned into soft shapes, whereas a deeper frill of 10 cm (4 in) can be bunched up and stitched in place to make a ruffle.

* A neat and attractive finish for a heading which does not need to be folded over - i.e bound or bound and lined, is a pocket heading which is pulled up with ribbon or rouleau.

* When calculating the fabric needed for each frill, you will need to allow for the required frill height, the same amount to return behind and then 1.5 cm (⅝ in) to take the gathering stitches. On a very few designs, the fabric will not need to return to the back - mainly if the heading has been piped and lined, bound, bound and lined, or finished with a shell or ribbon "hem".

* Once the gathers have been made, sit the cover over the under shade and adjust so that the cover fits easily and the frill stands or falls as you wish.

Curtain tape heading

If necessary, fold, press and pin the heading allowance to the inside.

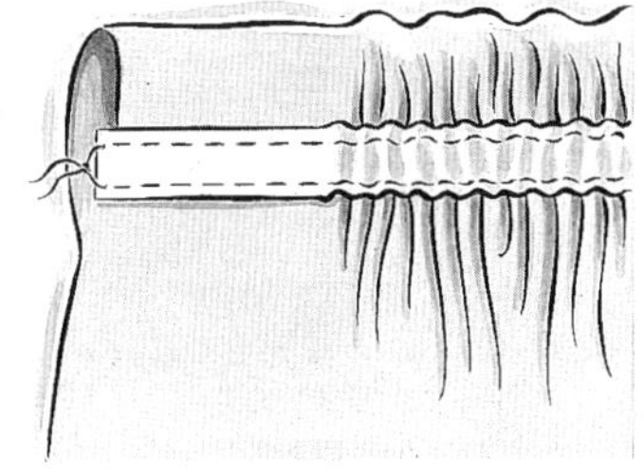

Pin curtain heading tape to the inside, measuring the frill depth down from the top of the shade to the top of the tape. Pin along the centre of the tape and across the tape. Knot one end to secure the cords and pull the cords at the other end free. Stitch along the outer edges, leaving the cross pins in place to keep the tape flat. Pull up to the required size and finish with a fabric-covered tape band (see below).

Hand-gathered heading

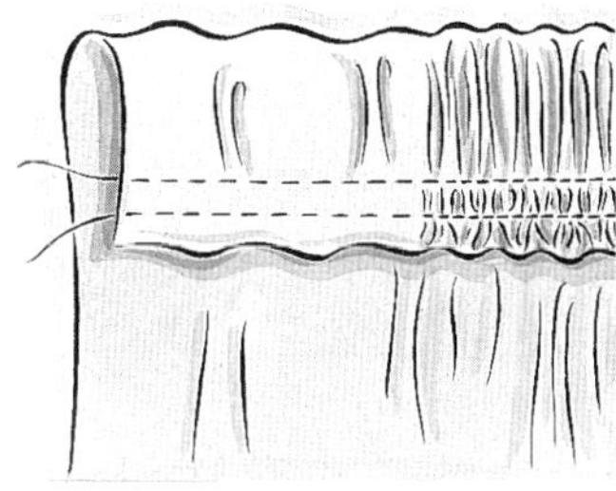

If necessary, fold, press and pin the heading allowance to the inside. Measure the frill depth and mark with pins at 10 - 15 cm (4 - 6 in) intervals. Run a gathering thread along this line and another just below the raw edge. Pull up to the required size and secure the threads. Make a fabric-covered tape band and stitch in place.

Fabric-covered tape band

Cut a length of calico, firm canvas or curtain buckram 1.5 cm (⅝ in) wide and the length of the finished top circumference. Cut a strip of fabric 3 cm (1¼ in) longer and 4 cm (1½ in) wide. Press the fabric strip over the calico strip to enclose.

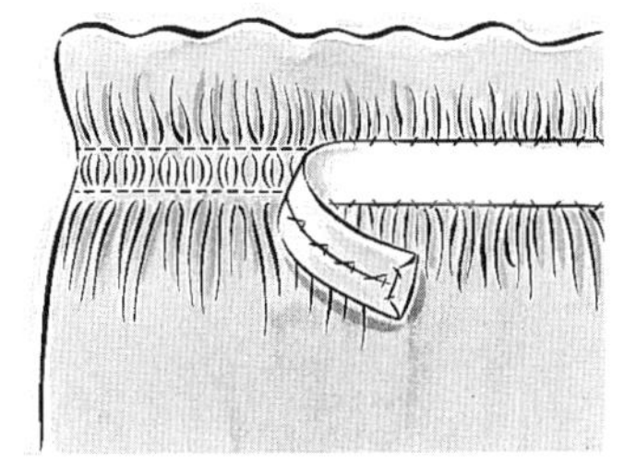

Herringbone the raw edges along the length and neaten one end. Spread the skirt gathers evenly and finger press straight. Mark the band into same number of divisions as the skirt. Pin the covered band over, enclosing all raw edges and threads. Stitch with small stitches along both sides, keeping the gathering pleats straight and evenly spaced.

Pocket heading

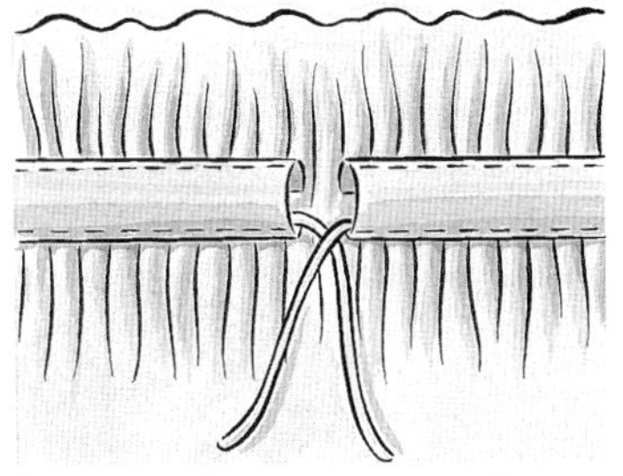

Cut a strip of same or contrast fabric 3 cm (1¼ in) wide and length equal to the skirt circumference.

Press long sides under, so that the band is now 1.5 cm (⅝ in) wide. Press both ends under neatly.

Pin this band to the front of the shade with the top of the band at the bottom of the frill depth.

Stitch close to each edge. Thread a length or ribbon, a cord or rouleau tie (see below) through and pull up to the required size.

ROULEAU TIES

Rouleaux can be as long and thin as cord, or wider and shorter to make bows in place of ribbon. Use a scrap of fabric or cord and tie loosely to determine the length and width the finished rouleau tie should be.

Cut a strip of fabric double the width of the finished rouleau times the length required plus 1 cm (⅜ in) seam allowances all round.

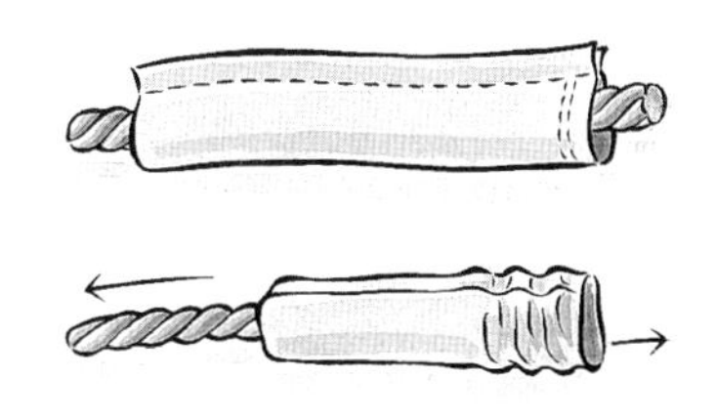

Press in half lengthwise, right sides together, enclosing a longer length of ribbon or piping cord. Double stitch across the top and down the long side 1 cm (⅜ in) from the raw edge. Trim the top corners and, using a pin, bring the outer fabric up and over the stitched end to start the rouleau going. Pull the cord now exposed from the bottom, sleeving the outer fabric upwards, until the cord has travelled through the channel and the rouleau is completely through, right side out.

Self-binding

Self-binding is a smart and elegant way to finish off a silk or cotton shade, where fabric has been stitched to a frame. Usually the frame will be lined and fitted, so that it is stitched to the front of both top and base rings.

*Fabric for self-bindings should be fine enough so that it can be folded into three without becoming bulky. Cut a small piece 5 cm (2 in) wide and fold to test. You might need your binding to be slightly wider or slightly narrower when finished, so adjust the cut width accordingly. Cuts must always be on the cross if the binding is to fit neatly round the curve of the frame.

1. Measure the circumferences of the top and base rings and cut two strips on the cross to this length plus seams allowances and approximately 5 cm (2 in) wide. These must be without joins. If you are short of fabric, it is better to use a purchased trimming or a contrast colour.

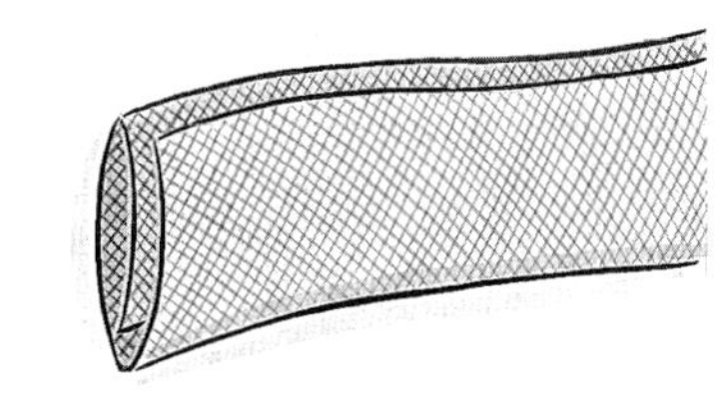

2. Press the strips in three lengthwise, so that the under piece finishes 2 mm (1/16 in) from the fold.
3. Starting at the back of the shade and lining up with one section, pin the binding to the frame, so that the shorter piece is against the shade fabric, right sides together.
4. Stitch all round, using lampshade stitches, starting and stopping 5 cm (2 in) from the end.
5. Pin the binding to join on the cross and stitch the seam with tiny hand stitches. Trim back the seam and finger press flat.
6. Stitch the remaining joined section of the binding to the frame. Fold over the binding to conceal the stitches and slipstitch in place.

MAKING A TEMPLATE

To design and place motifs and border designs for card and for fabric shades, to make more elaborate fabric shade covers with tucks and pleats, gores and inset sections, first a template needs to be made to the exact size of the under shade, then a toile or template to the exact size of the finished shade. In this way you can experiment with different placements, section sizes, fullness and ideas without risking the much more valuable top fabric. Calico (or any firmly woven fabric), stencil acetate or dressmaker's pattern paper may be used to make the template.

1. Place your material over an existing shade if you are to copy, or over the under shade if you are to cover. Pin along the existing seam line. Trim away to approximately 2 cm (¾ in) top and bottom. If you can't pin into the shade itself, push pins through just above the top ring and just below the bottom ring. Secure at intervals with small pieces of masking tape. When the template is quite tight, pencil along the seam and rings. Remove the fabric and cut out along the pencil lines.

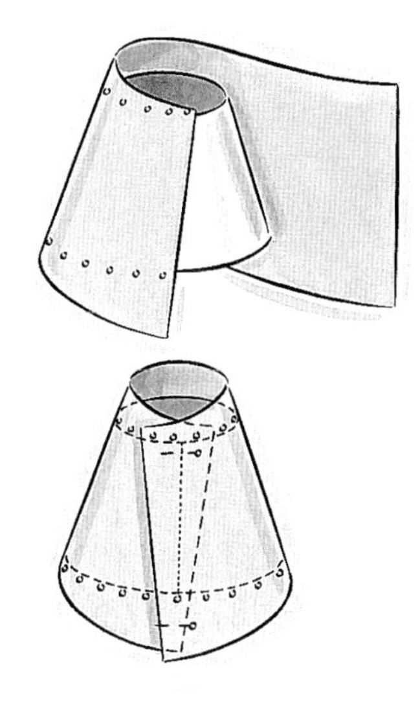

2. Keep this template for future reference and make a copy onto another piece of paper or calico, whichever is relevant.
3. This pattern can then be made up into a calico toile with all details pencilled on or cut out and all seam allowances added. Tacked together, the shade or shade cover can be tested for fit and fullness before cutting the top fabric. Instructions with individual projects specify how it can be used to make more complex designs.

Standard empire

Pembroke

Coolie

Conic empire

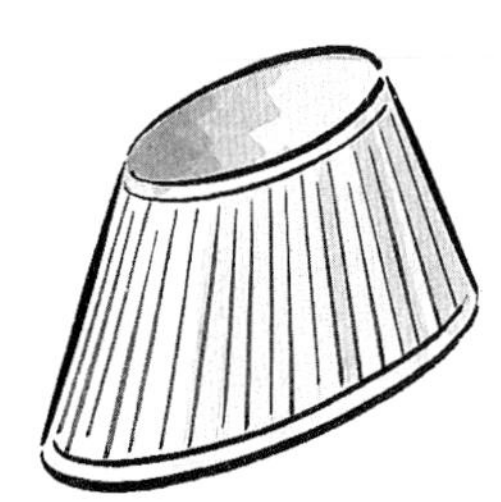

Oval empire

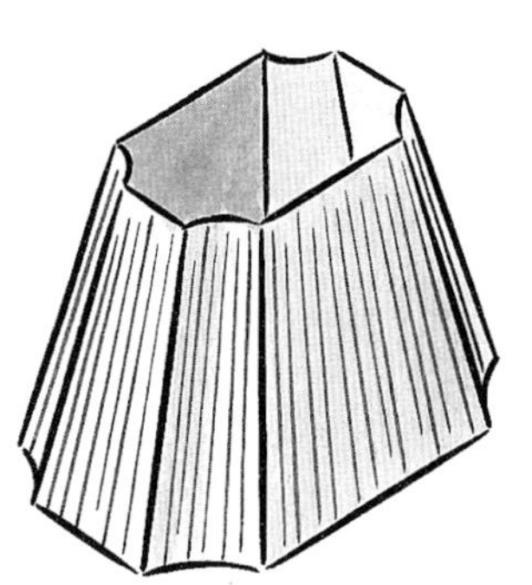

Regency

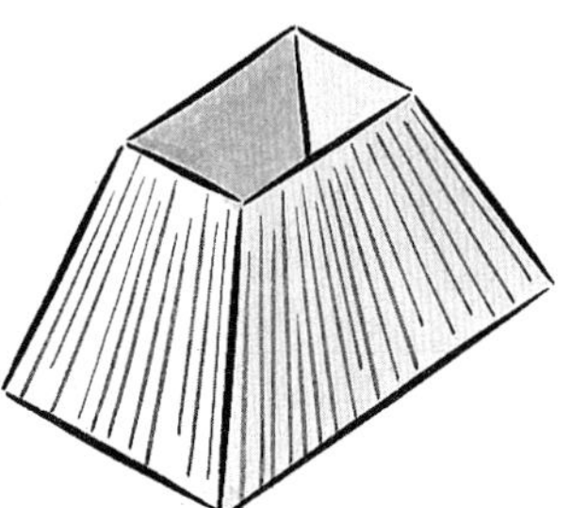

Straight rectangle

Half

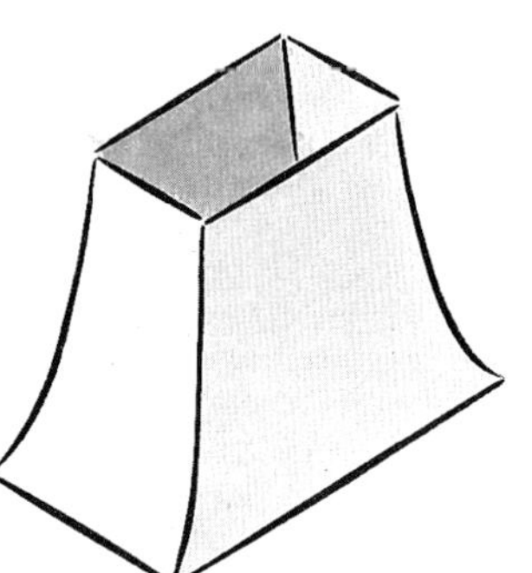

Bowed rectangle

Candle

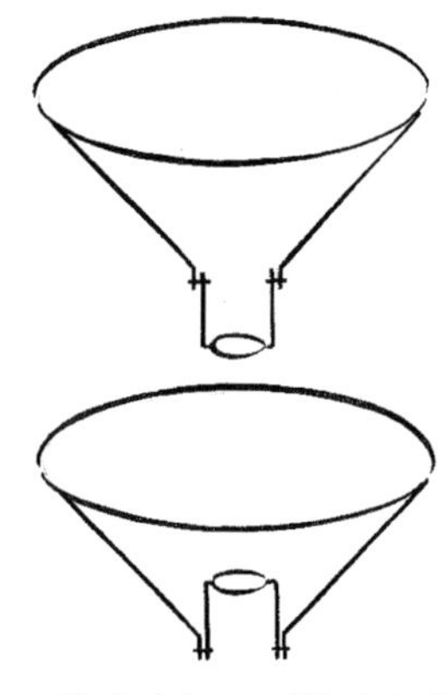

Gimbal (reversible joint)

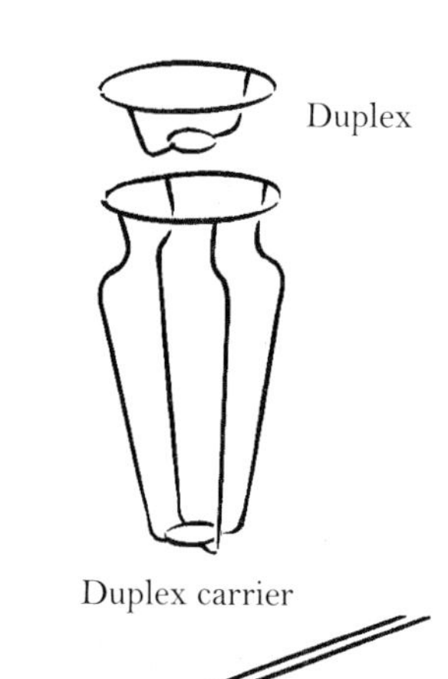

Duplex

Duplex carrier

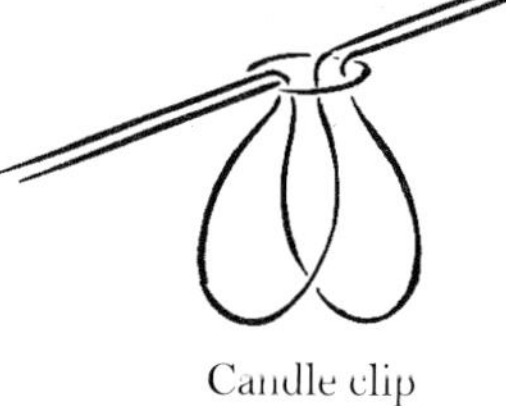

Candle clip

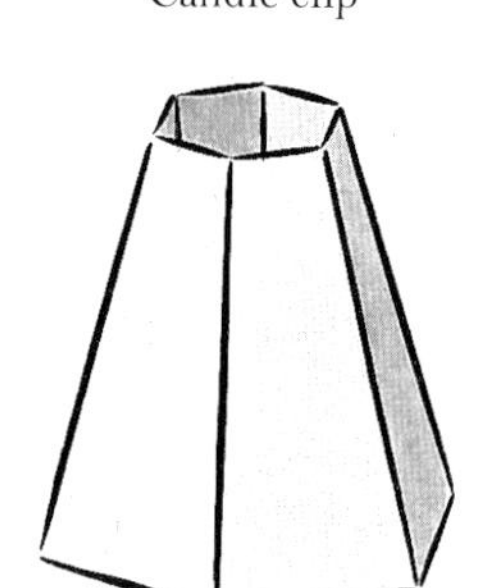

Hexagon

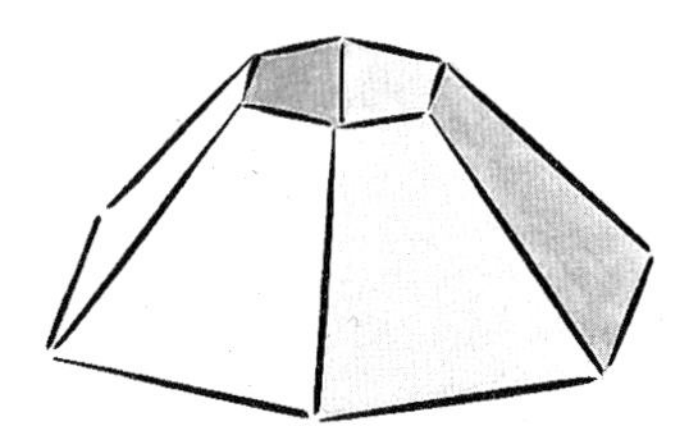

Hexagonal coolie

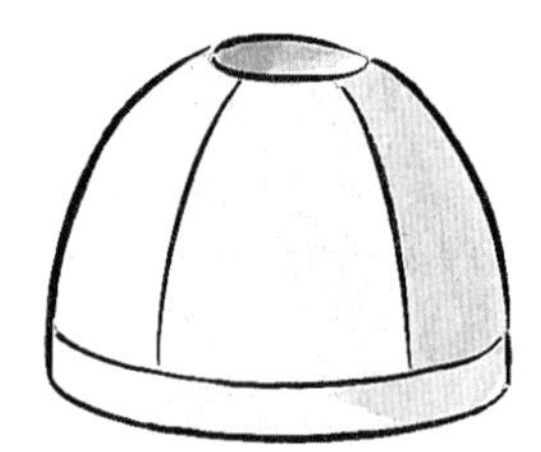

Galleried dome

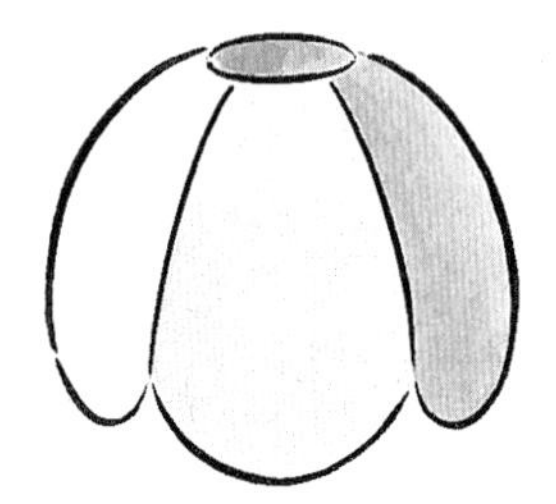

Scalloped dome

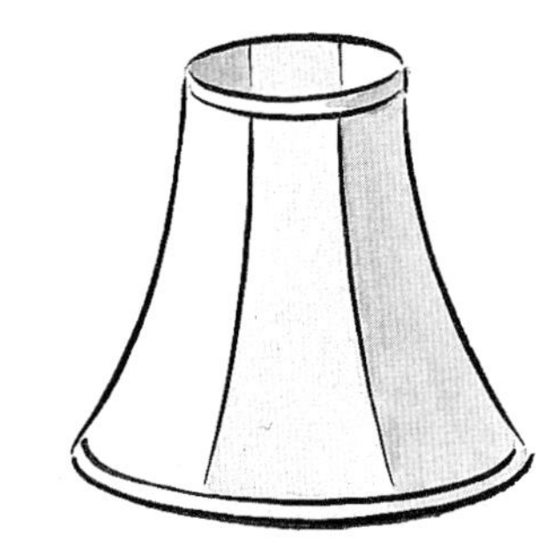

Bowed empire

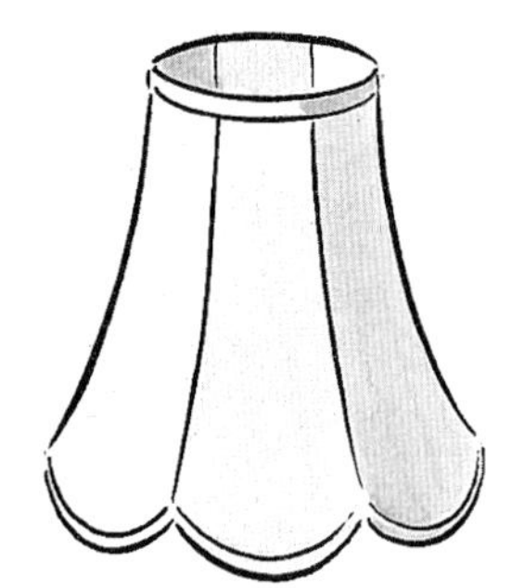

Scalloped bowed empire

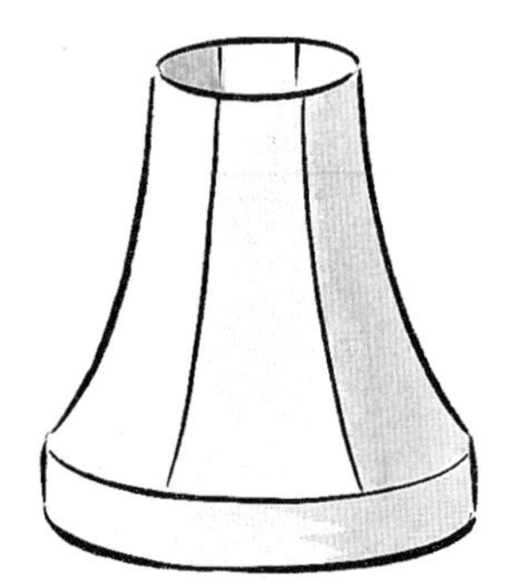

Bowed empire with collar

FRAME SIZES AND MATERIALS CHARTS

Shade frames fall into two main categories: those with side struts suitable for fabric covering and those with separate rings, which hold card or stiffened fabric at the top and base only. Most shades can have most fitting types. Reversible gimbal fittings are ideal for smaller shades, which can then fit over a side lamp or hang from a ceiling lamp.

Large lampshades for table lamps and standard lamps will be more secure with a duplex fitting at the top of the shade, resting on a duplex shade support which fits to the base. Bulb clips are available in sizes to fit small and larger golf ball bulbs or candle bulbs.

FRAME SIZES *(inches)*

Cooolie			Pembroke			Empire			Candle		
base	*top*	*slope*	*base*	*top*	*slope*	*base*	*top*	*slope*	*base*	*top*	*slope*
8	3	5	8	5	6	8	4	6	6	3	5
9	3½	5½	9	6	7	9	4½	6½	7	3	5
10	4	6	10	6	7	10	5	7	8	3	5½
11	4	6½	11	6½	8	11	5	7½	10	3	6
12	4	7	12	7	8½	12	6	8	12	3	7
13	4½	7½	13	8	9	13	6½	8½			
14	4½	8	14	9	9	14	7	9			
15	5	8½	16	11	11	16	8	10			
16	5	9	18	12	12	18	9½	12			
17	5½	9½	20	13	13	20	10	13			
18	6	10	22	14	14	22	11	14			
20	6	11	24	16	16	24	12	16			

FRAME SIZES *(centimetres)*

Cooolie			Pembroke			Empire			Candle		
base	*top*	*slope*	*base*	*top*	*slope*	*base*	*top*	*slope*	*base*	*top*	*slope*
20	7.5	12.5	20	12.5	15	20	10	15	15	7.5	12.5
23	8.5	14	23	15	18	23	11.5	16.5	18	7.5	12.5
25	10	15	25	15	18	25	12.5	18	20	7.5	14
28	10	16.5	28	16.5	20	28	12.5	19	25	7.5	15
30	10	18	30	18	21.5	30	15	20	30	7.5	18
33	11.5	19	33	20	23	33	16.5	21.5			
35.5	11.5	20	35.5	23	23	35.5	18	23			
38	12.5	21.5	40	28	28	40	20	25			
40	12.5	23	45.5	30	30	45.5	24	30			
43	14	24	51	33	33	51	25	33			
45.5	15	25	56	35.5	35.5	56	28	35.5			
51	15	28	61	40	40	61	30	40			

CANDLE SHADES/CARD

to fit standard holder *(inches)*

base	*top*	*slope*
3½	2½	4
4	2½	4
4½	2½	4
5	2½	4
5½	2½	4½
6	2½	5
7	2½	5

CANDLE SHADES

to fit standard holder *(centimetres)*

base	*top*	*slope*
9	5	10
10	5	10
11.5	5	10
12.5	5	10
14	5	11.5
15	5	12.5
18	5	12.5

To help you to identify the frame and style, some of the most used standard shapes are illustrated on the previous page.

Each shade can have variations, e.g. a bowed hexagonal empire with scalloped top; a conic empire with a square top, and most variations are available to order from a lampshade specialist.

Each manufacturer has his or her own frame sizes, my preferred ones are listed below. Shade sizes are always listed by base, top and slope measurements, corresponding to letters A, B and C on the measuring diagrams throughout the book. Fabric quantities for specific projects have been given for even numbers only on the relevant pages.

BASES

Almost anything can make a lamp base, whether an old tea caddy, an earthenware pot or a piece of precious porcelain. The only thing that really matters is that the shade fits the base and that the whole is the right size for its position in the room. As a rule of thumb, the diameter of the shade should be at least as much as the bottom of the base to the top of the neck. Of course, this does not apply when a candle shade sits atop a 60 or 90 cm (24 or 36 in) slender stand but rules can always be broken once you have trained your eye. Practise positioning lamps higher or lower than you normally might and study the effect. Balance a picture behind or an ornament to one side to judge which best suits the particular setting for the shade.

Index

A

All in one (box pleated), 21

B

Bandana edging (box pleated), 23
Basic party shade, 72
Beaded pleats (box pleated), 21
Bee appliqué, 58
Binding a corner, 124
Binding the frame, 122
Binding, 124
Black velvet slipcover
(winter warmers), 119
Blanket stitch, 123
Bobble-trimmed slipcover
(whiter than white), 93
Bordered hem
(summer garden), 104
Box pleated shade, 20
Butterfly edging
Butterfly edging
(summer garden), 105
Buttoned gored shade
(whiter than white), 94
Buttoned slipcover
(whiter than white), 93
Buttonhole stitch, 123

C

Calico-covered card shade, 40
Card templates, 42-43
Child's birthday candle shade
template, 66
Christmas candle shade, 64
Classic linen shade (stretched), 14
Contrast pintucks, 112
Coolie shade (stretched), 15
Covered seams, 12
Curtain tape heading, 124

D

Decorative bows, 73
Decorative roses, 73
Double frilled hem pleated
and gathered), 35
Double layers
(summer garden), 105
Double-skirted slipcover shade
with pointed collar
(whiter than white), 90

E

Easter candle candle shade
template, 66
Edgings gallery (pleated
and gathered), 31

F

Fabric-covered card shade, 40
Fabric-covered tape band, 124
Facings, 123
Fan edging (pleated and
gathered), 31
Flared skirt (evening dress), 85
Flower card template
(pinpricked and pierced), 51
French seam, 124
Frilled edge (pleated and
gathered), 31
Frilled edge, stretched shade, 14
Frilled headings, 124
curtain tape heading, 125
fabric-covered tape band, 125
hand-gathered heading, 125
pocket heading, 125
Full length pintucks, 114

G

Gored and buttoned slipcover
(evening dress), 81
Gored slipcover shade
(evening dress), 78
Gored slipcover shade with lid
(evening dress), 79

H

Hand-gathered heading, 124
Handmade fringing (pleated
and gathered), 31
Hemming stitch, 123
Hems, 124
shell hemming, 124
Herringbone stitch, 123
Hexagonal frame with fringe
(stretched), 15
Hole-punched felt slipcover
(winter warmers), 121

J

Joining piping, 124

L

Lampshade stitch, 123
Lined shades (summer garden), 105
Linings, 122
pleated, 122
tight, 122
Making a template, 125
Mock box pleats, 22

O

Oak leaf and acorn shade
(pinpricked and pierced), 52
Oak leaf and acorn template
(pinpricked and pierced), 52
One-piece shade (pleated
and gathered), 33
Oval shade (card), 44

P

Patterned fabric shade
(pinpricked and pierced), 50
Petal template (evening dress), 82
Petal-trimmed slipcover
(evening dress), 83
Pink roses (whiter than white), 92
Pinning gathered fabric, 123
Pinning piping, 124
Pinning, 123
Piped flared slipcover
(evening dress), 81
Piping, 124
pinning piping, 124
Pleated and gathered empire, 28
Pleated heading
(summer garden), 105
Pleated lining, 122
Pleated shade (card), 46
Pleated shade with pom pom
tassels, 30
Pocket heading, 124
Pointed collar template, 92
Preparing the frame, 122
binding the frame, 122
Pressing, 124

Q

Quick felt slipcover
(winter warmers), 119

R

Ribbon edges, 73
Rouleau ties, 125
Ruched heading
(summer garden), 104

S

Safety, 122
Scalloped candle shade
template, 66-67
Scalloped edges (card), 41
Seams, 124
flat, 124
French, 124
pressing, 124
Self-binding, 125
Self-bound edges (pleated and
gathered), 31
Shell hemming, 124
Shot silk slipcover
(evening dress), 84
Shot taffeta pintucks, 114
Simple flared cover
(whiter than white), 94
Single mock box pleats, 23
Square shade (card), 44
Square throwover with bee
appliqué, 58
Standard lamp
(whiter than white), 87
Stencil design, 120
Stitched seams, 13
Stitches, 123
blanket, 123
buttonhole, 123
hemming, 123
herringbone, 123
lampshade, 123

T

Taffeta pintucks and pearls, 110
Taped edges (card), 41
Tartan slipcover
(winter warmers), 118
Templates:
card, 42-43
child's birthday candle shade
template, 66
Easter candle candle shade
template, 66
flower card template, 51
oak leaf and acorn template, 52
petal template, 82
pointed collar template, 92
scalloped candle shade
template, 66-67
Thanksgiving candle shade
template, 67
Valentine's Day candle shade
template, 67
Thanksgiving candle shade
template, 67
Tight lining, 122
Traditional stretched cover, 12
Triple-skirted and gathered
slipcover (summer garden), 100
Twisted roll (pleated and
gathered), 32
Two-layered skirt (evening
dress), 82
Two-toned cut fringing (pleated
and gathered), 31

V

Valentine's Day candle
shade template, 67
Violets (summer garden), 102

W

Wall shade (pleated and
gathered), 29

Z

Zebra-skin ribbon slipcover
(whiter than white), 93